The Vegeterranean

ITALIAN VEGETARIAN COOKING

INSIDE THE KITCHEN OF THE COUNTRY HOUSE MONTALI

Malu Simões & Alberto Musacchio

The Vegeterranean

ITALIAN VEGETARIAN COOKING

INSIDE THE KITCHEN OF THE COUNTRY HOUSE MONTALI

Written with Grace Choi

❖

Photography & Design by David Piening

SIMON &
SCHUSTER

London · New York · Sydney · Toronto

First published in Great Britain by Simon & Schuster UK Ltd, 2008
A CBS Company

Simon & Schuster UK Ltd
Africa House, 64–78 Kingsway, London WC2B 6AH

1 3 5 7 9 10 8 6 4 2

Printed in Italy

ISBN 978-1-84737-195-9

TABLE OF CONTENTS

ACKNOWLEDGEMENTS

It has been about ten years since people asked us to write a cookery book. This, of course, sounds like an honour but it becomes one of those things that you should do and never end up doing: a kind of 'memento' of something you keep forgetting or postponing. Surely nothing to do with the typical Italian attitude of being precise and punctual and never postponing things! My major problem indeed was, and still is, language.

To write any book, even a cookery one, requires a perfect mastery of the language in which you write. I do speak a small number of languages apart from Italian, but none good enough to allow me to write a book – and definitely not English. A cookery book, moreover, uses very technical terminology that I was not really sure I was willing to study. When we finally decided to embark on this project, language as a concept became a big part of the game. The English reader's edition of this book, in fact, has been an amusing international mixture of British ounces and liquid ounces, checked with grams and kilos, then translated into American cups and finally re-checked to match medieval Italian culinary traditions! A new kind of language indeed.

We also extensively discussed the different accent and 'parfume' that the writing should have. "Should we give it an English accent or an American one?" "Should we say courgette or zucchini?" "Bruschetta or bruscetta?" "Aubergine or eggplants?" These have often been the strange conversations we had amongst a Korean-American writer, a Brazilian chef, an Italian entrepreneur, a Slovakian sous-chef and an English journalist friend who gave us hints on the 'pronunciation' of the book! The major problem that even Grace could not solve, neither using her American accent nor even trying a good British version, was regarding my own writing. We all thought it would be ridiculous to 'hear' an Italian speaking 'English'. Finally we decided to let my writing stand and just apologize for the mistakes.

We also did some other food language research. Proposing mostly Italian food (even with a wider international touch) to English and American people, may not be easy if you really want the reader to be able to reproduce your recipes. We decided to keep most of the Italian regional recipes as close to the old original ones as possible. Since Italian food has become so widely popular abroad, people have ended up seeing Italian pizzas being made with pineapple and ham. No Italian would ever eat a pizza with pineapple and ham! We really wanted to stick to the original source of the culinary tradition.

But the next language question was "How can I teach a British person to cook something with Castelmagno cheese?" when we know Castelmagno is one of the rarest and most expensive cheeses in our country. We decided to keep the original recipes with all the original ingredients, but also give possible variations for any uncommon ingredients. The recipe will say Castelmagno, but it will also suggest what other kind of cheese might take its place. We gave quick hints for Vegans as well. These were just the first stages of the main work.

To start from the beginning, in January 2005, my wife, Malu, and I were reading Grace Choi's CV, and found her application very interesting. Grace is a young American-Korean chef who has studied at the French Culinary Institute of New York and later trained in one of the best restaurants in all the USA. When we began reading her application to come and work at Montali as an apprentice, we both noticed her 'magna cum laude' BA from the University of Notre Dame. She had studied a lot in her life. But what grabbed our attention even more was a sentence in her CV in which she stated how in love she was with food writing.

This was exactly who we were looking for, someone who could be a good chef, but was also capable of writing about food. Because we were still thinking about how to face the language problem of a book, here might be the answer to our problem. After we e-mailed, Grace decided to come and work here. The first few months were dedicated to her learning our recipes and working hard in the kitchen. Later she worked more and more on writing and typing the recipes and the stories of this book.

never giving up, never getting sick, never leaving the job, never less than perfect: a true professional in the kitchen. Daniel Sharp helped Janko and all of us in the kitchen with his incomparable sense of humour, cheering everyone up. David Piening used his excellent skill in giving life with his camera to all those

Her excellent knowledge of the language, her great will power and her natural sense of humour definitely helped a lot in drafting the book.

That is how the book started to come to life... with team work that lasted most of the summer of 2005. My wife was in charge of the recipes, of course. To keep the kitchen perfectly organized became quite a hard job as the photography required an enormous effort – just when we needed to produce the food for the clients. Malu ran like never before in her life. Grace typed everything down and wrote some of the biographical stories. I wrote some others.

The faithful sous-chef, Jan Bodnar, took charge of the kitchen when everyone was getting angry with the photography and plate setting. He has been with us for five long years, the only one

splendid recipes. It is because of his expertise that the food will seem to pop out of these colourful pages. Bonaria, Alena, Marketa, Sylvia, Giannina and Giuliana helped to run the hotel even when everyone else was busy with sauces and cameras. A deep thanks to all those splendid guys for having worked so hard.

And a deep thanks to all the wonderful clients who have always believed in the Country House Montali, who have returned and supported such a difficult business, and also for suggesting this wonderful book. Special thanks to ATAL for supplying the elegant chinaware that made these images possible and to my brother, Gianni, for the spectacular art that served as the backdrop for many of the shots.

Alberto Musacchio

When I arrived at the Country House Montali on March 26 of 2005, the stillness of the Umbrian countryside and the winding dirt roads leading to the hotel were the first to take my notice. I stood in the centre of the twenty-five-acre property with a crystal clear view of Lake Trasimeno, comparing my new surroundings with my old ones. Perfectly aligned olive trees replaced the skyscrapers of Manhattan; verdant greens spanned the mountain plateau in the same manner that yellow taxicabs flood Times Square. The hushed tranquillity was more overwhelming than the sounds of ambulances, trucks and blaring horns that I had grown quite accustomed to. Sharp senses returned to my nose as I picked up the scent of fresh-cut grass with a flutter of rosemary and mint from the herb garden.

an inimitability that arrives with the rare combination of rustic Italian cooking techniques and the exclusive use of vegetarian products.

From the beginning of my seven-month journey with Alberto Musacchio, Malu Simões and the kitchen and waiting staff, I knew that Montali was not simply a hotel that provided rooms and hot meals. It was the home of countless stories and memories, a gathering of remarkable individuals pursuing incredible dreams, a kitchen that held years of laughter, wine, dancing, spices and music. At the end of every day, each dish that we contributed to as a family exuded passions and new histories. In the same light, the Montali cookbook could not be a simple index of recipes and techniques. As no guest leaves Montali

While the serenity of the hotel and its surroundings offer a haven to both local and international guests, the gourmet vegetarian cuisine is what leaves the greatest impression. After twenty-five years of refining recipes and menu combinations in compliance with seasonal fruits and vegetables, the dishes exude not only incredible flavours and textures, but also

without experiencing something even more of the beauty of the Italian countryside and the fulfilment of a delicious four-course dinner, no reader should finish this book without having got to know Alberto, Malu and the spirit of the kitchen staff.

Grace Choi

The reason why the Country House Montali has a relatively good culinary reputation is that, for a long time, it has produced an unusual gourmet vegetarian cuisine. From a fine dining point of view, vegetarianism has never really fully developed, probably due to the difficulties of using a relatively small number of ingredients and also avoiding some particularly succulent ones, like most of the animal fats.

Starting with a restaurant in Perugia we ended in the countryside of Umbria where we run our resort. For more than two decades, in fact, we have been involved in trying to give vegetarian food a better interpretation and a more professional image. A bit of pride is present, I admit, as the challenge has been quite tough at times.

When they start any kind of business in India, they always begin by singing the praises of Lord Ganesha, the elephant-headed god, as he is the tutor, lord of goodwill and helper of 'starting things'. He is always the first one to be worshipped. The little culinary success and gratifications we have had would never have been possible without the help of the person who first opened the fine dining horizon to us: our first Japanese chef Akira Shishido. As he has been the embodiment of Lord Ganesha to us, we would like to start this book by referring to him.

At this time, 25 years ago, we were running a successful pub in the lovely city of Perugia. The town is a place crowded with young foreign students, flocking to study the Italian language in the biggest university for foreigners in the country. This pub was just an attempt to make some money and have as much fun as possible, with lots of sleepless nights and enjoying 'la dolce vita' as young entrepreneurial bohemians. I was 19.

With no intention of producing any gourmet cuisine, we made good, vegetarian food to feed the hoards of hungry young clients. Among the

different ethnic groups who were populating our international pub were quite a large number of Japanese. Surely one of the most educated groups, Japanese people have always been in love with elegant Italian cars, clothes and in general any special fashion and architectural

designer trend. As pub customers, they were very respectful, well educated and, most importantly for the host, big drinkers.

I remember how they introduced me, for the first time, to a trick, surely of imperial origin, that allowed them to drink more alcohol than any strong and healthy human being should have been capable of! They were not drinking glasses of wine or a few light beers but quantities of whisky – enough to fill a few lorries. The trick that they were using consisted of literally swallowing a tablespoon of pure olive oil before starting a drinking night . The big spoon of oil lined the gastric membrane, allowing the gentlemen to consume a much larger quantity of alcohol. By the end of the evening, the alcohol was producing its consequences anyway... and they were generally devastating!!! I imagine the Emperor and his concubines originally used some horrible fish oil, but the modern Japanese 'ex pat' had found the noble olive juice more tasty and established it as their 'modern time muse'.

Whisky, certainly a big source of income for our business, was always available, so that on the arrival of the Japanese we had a large stock of Scotch and spoonfuls of olive oil ready in the kitchen. In all, it was a good time because they weren't creating the problems of some other nationalities, who usually tended to vent the effect of their whisky in horrible and noisy fights, so often found in night time places. Not the Japanese. I would imagine that anyone who started a fight after a drinking session with his Emperor would have been asked to commit hara-kiri – after first being told to clean up the mess in the restaurant!

Nevertheless we started to hide, if not the whisky then the olive oil, when one day dear Yasugi, an old client of ours, staggering with an excess of alcohol, decided to grab the long stove pipe (lit up) that ran all around the restaurant. The faces of the unfortunate customers who saw and heard a dozen metres of very hot, and very dirty, stove pipe falling, with the fire still lit and smoke filling up the whole restaurant, remained in our memories for a long time. From then on we made absolutely sure that no hara-kiri knives were present (and we started to hide the olive oil as well).

And there, in the middle of this crowd of bohemian Japanese, maybe the epitome of a very sophisticated class of intellectual artists, stood the good Akira. A chef by birth, he was one of the few persons born under the sign of cooking and surely appointed to the celebrity of international fine dining. I can say now, 25 years later, that only some people choose the job of a chef because it is very

hard. Few keep loving the job. Very few are predestined to it. There are just some who have a karmic affinity to the kitchen itself. Akira was one of those.

He was the kind of chef who, the more he was under pressure, the more he loved to work. Working satisfaction for Akira was a busy night in which, after much work and a therefore empty kitchen, a big crowd of people would pop up from some late night theatre in large numbers, all very hungry. All of us were like "Oh shit!". Akira, on the other hand, loved to feed people without anything in the kitchen except his creativity. To work hard was not enough for him. What Akira was longing for was ....challenge.

That was the reason that he left a nice job in a five star restaurant to come and work for us in a less than ordinary place. He thought vegetarian food would be a big challenge because it is one of the most difficult cuisines in the world. He simply took the challenge. The night in which we offered him a job in our place, of course, we took out the olive oil spoon and a big stock of whisky to try to convince him. But he was much too clever, even under the influence of alcohol, and managed to start giving out rules to everybody in the restaurant right away, even though he had just accepted the job. Later on, we discovered that the process of hiring a great chef was not easy at all. Chefs are renowned for moodiness and temperamental attitudes...and Akira was a great chef!

Even for us proprietors, life became much harder. Although the big success that our place had (mostly due to having been in the proper place at the proper time with a proper product) continued, our only interests until that moment had been partying without any particular real professionality. Cooking and serving drinks were just a means to get the lifestyle.

All of a sudden things changed. I still remember the many times in which I was reproached for some small detail in serving Akira's food. One

time he even refused to heat some rice because I spent a bit of time talking with a client who had asked me a question, and consequently the rice lost its temperature. "You go and heat it yourself" was his answer – and I was supposed to be the boss!!! But then came the satisfaction of doing something with a lot of attention and care. More and more, we started to love what we were doing. On top of everything, Akira was joining the two best culinary and serving traditions in the world: the Japanese with its concept of beauty and great presentation and the Italian with its culinary pride and flamboyance.

I do not know, in the 25 following years, having personally trained dozens of young men and women to cook and wait tables, how many times I have remembered my first guru in this wonderful world of fine dining, and his teachings on how to make a client feel at home and welcome in a place. And I have always remembered them with the greatest pleasure and respect.

I have realised that there is a last 'karmic' stage that allows a cook, even from an excellent cookery school, to become a real chef. Few are, in fact, chefs who will not always repeat the same few recipes they know but will keep exploring, with willingness and pleasure, the secret world of hidden flavours. Very few will be chefs who will enjoy feeding a crowd, late at night, with an empty kitchen. But that is how a chef has to be.

This chapter is a homage to Akira Shishido, who literally kicked us in the direction of gourmet cuisine. Unfortunately I have lost track of him, but I am sure success has smiled on him – it would be impossible for it to be any different.

Ingredienti & Tecniche

INGREDIENTS & TECHNIQUES

A FEW THINGS TO KEEP IN MIND WHEN READING THIS BOOK

· This book has been divided into four courses in the likeness of a typical Country House Montali dinner. First are the Antipasti (starters), then the Primi (first courses), followed by the Secondi (second courses), and finally the Dolci (desserts).

· Wine has been paired with a number of recipes, specifically the Primi as is the Italian tradition.

· Where possible, ingredients have been given in both metric and Imperial measurements.

· Vegan and gluten-free recipes are available for some recipes.

· Sauces and creams are found in the Basics section. While they are referred to within this book, they are also excellent with an array of other dishes as so desired.

· Ingredients have been listed in the order in which they are used.

 Ⓔ = Easy   Ⓜ = Medium   Ⓓ = Difficult

INGREDIENTS

Olive Oil
'Extra virgin' olive oil, the cold-pressed result of the first pressing of olives. At 1% acid, it is the highest quality of olive oil and the only variety that should be used.

Eggs
Generally medium-sized, approximately 50 g (1½ oz).

Single Cream
A dense cream with the consistency of crème fraîche.

Double Cream
Also known as heavy or whipping cream.

Milk
Always whole milk.

Butter
Always unsalted.

Vanilla
Generally in the form of vanilla extract unless the recipe specifies vanilla beans.

Italian '00' Flour
Used for light and airy baking. Can be replaced with regular flour if necessary.

Manitoba Flour

Unbleached, high gluten flour. Develops a high quantity of gluten during the kneading and cooking process, resulting in a chewy bread. Can be substituted with bread flour.

Grano Duro Flour

A fine semolina flour, otherwise known as durum flour or durum wheat flour.

Semolina Flour

A coarser durum wheat flour used in puddings, soups and pastas like *Gnocchi alla Romana*.

Cornstarch

Also known as cornflour. Not to be confused with cornmeal or polenta. Commonly used as a thickener.

Yeast

If the fresh variety is impossible to find, replace with a good quality dry active yeast, not instant.

Sugar

Caster/castor or granulated sugar.

Icing Sugar

Also known as confectioner's sugar.

Mosto Cotto or Saba

Grape juice reduction, also known to be the historical basis of balsamic vinegar. This syrup can be substituted with a normal syrup if difficult to find. During the off-season, Malu makes her own batch out of freshly pressed grape juice. To make at home, simmer 1 litre (1¼ pint) of grape juice over low heat until it is reduced to a tenth of the original quantity. Cool completely and keep in an airtight container for up to 1 year.

Rocket

A bitter green salad leaf, also known as arugula in the USA.

Mushrooms

Porcini, cremini, oyster or button mushrooms. If using dry porcini, rinse them in hot water till soft.

Pumpkin

Kabocha squash in the USA.

Radicchio

A purple-coloured lettuce, characteristically bitter. Great in salads as well as grilled, sautéed or baked.

Tahini

A thick sesame seed paste originating from the Middle East.

CHEESES

Charles de Gaulle on France: "How can one rule a country that produces more than 300 varieties of cheeses?"
Italy has more than 600! That's probably why Italians are so eclectically independent.

Castelmagno

A cow's cheese from its namesake in Piedmont where it is famously produced thousands of metres above sea level. Aged from 2 to 6 months in natural caves. The younger variety is very crumbly in texture and delicate in flavour. The aged version is sharper and spicier in taste. Legend says that, due to the cold, they make the cheese ferment under warm cow dung, thankfully with some straw in between!

Fontina

A mild cow's milk cheese produced in the Alps. The cows for this particular cheese graze on the highlands of northern Italy and the result is a strong and distinctive flavour. Used much in northern dishes like fonduta and risotto, and complements fruit and honey for a dessert.

Formaggio di Fossa

A distinct sheep's milk cheese from the Appenine of Marche region. Sometimes blended with cow's milk and goat's milk, it is left to age in underground caves due to the controlled humidity. The cheeses are kept in white cloth bags from 3 to 6 months while they lose water and fat. This fermentation process is what yields the particular flavour. Perfect by itself, alongside a *Secondi*, or with fruit and honey.

Mascarpone

A soft creamy cow's milk cheese and a must for the perfect Tiramisu.

Montasio

A cow's milk cheese (mild or aged varieties) commonly found in the Veneto region of northeast Italy. The younger variety is milder and slightly acidic, while the more aged types can be grated on top of pasta or served in wedges to complement the smokiness of grilled food.

Mozzarella

Most commonly made from cow's milk, produced in the southern regions of Campania, Puglia and Lazio. This fresh light cheese should be consumed within 3 days of buying. The buffalo variety comes from buffalo's milk and has a more distinct flavour and is very creamy. Delicious melted on top of pasta.

Parmigiano Reggiano

The 'king of cheeses,' this cow's milk cheese is famously produced in the city of Parma where it is aged for 24 months. The strong flavour is perfect for final touches, grated on top of pasta and mixed in at the last minute in several dishes. To produce a 56 kg (123 lb) whole Parmigiano requires 700 litres (1231 pints) of milk!!

Grana Padano Parmesan

Aged 12 months and milder than Parmigiano Reggiano. Its versatility allows it to be used in several dishes.

Pecorino di Pienza

One of the best pecorino cheeses from the small medieval town called Pienza, this sheep's milk cheese is known in Italy for its milder, soft flavour.

Pecorino Romano

A flaky, aged, salty sheep's cheese, used in pesto and sauces and grated on top of salads and pasta.

Robiola

A fresh creamy cheese made from milk from cows, sheep or goats, well known for its particular aroma and flavour. Wonderful spread on top of toasted bread or on a fruit and cheese platter.

Scamorza

A low-moisture, firm, dried mozzarella, also available in a smoked variety. Delicious when melted on top of your favourite foods.

Taleggio

A sweet, lightly acidic cheese from cow's milk originally from Val Taleggio in Lombardia, northern Italy. The delicate aroma resembles that of the truffle. Delicious as an accompaniment to fruit or as a base to a sauce. Buy fresh and consume within 6 days. This is one of the few cheeses that freezes well.

TECHNIQUES

Blackening Bell Peppers

Place a bell pepper on a baking tray and cook at Gas Mark 4/180°C/350°F for 40 minutes or until the pepper has blackened. Remove from the oven, place the pepper in a plastic bag, seal and leave for at least 30 minutes or until cooled. Remove from the bag and peel. Cut off the stem, open and cut into desired pieces.

Boiling and Peeling Potatoes

Place washed potatoes in a pot and cover with lightly salted cool water. Bring to a boil and cook until tender. Remove the potatoes with a slotted spoon one at a time. Pierce with a fork and hold with one hand while peeling with a knife in the other.

Deep Frying

When deep frying, pour enough vegetable oil into a heavy-bottomed pot or large pan to submerge whatever you intend to fry. Depending on the dish, there are two ways to test the proper heat of oil for deep frying. When cooking vegetables like aubergines or dough-based dishes like Calzoni, place a small piece of bread in the hot oil, allowing the bread to sizzle. When the bread becomes still and unmoving, the oil is ready. For batter-based deep frying, drop a small amount of batter into the hot oil. If the batter drops to the bottom and immediately rises to the top, the oil is hot enough. If the batter lingers at the bottom for even a second, the oil is not ready. When deep frying, always place the food in the oil at a close distance to avoid splatter.

If you notice that, in either test, the bread or batter browns very quickly, turn down the heat or remove the pot to cool down the oil.

Flambéing

Towards the end of sautéing, remove the pan from the high heat but leave the flame on. Pour a fine quality liquor like cognac or brandy into the pan and place back on the heat, holding the pan at a tilt so that the flame from the stove can ignite the alcohol. Be sure to stand back because the flames will rise rapidly and then die down after a few seconds.

Ice Baths

In order to abruptly stop the cooking of food, or rapidly cool down stocks and sauces, many recipes will call for an ice bath.

Fill a large bowl with cold water and cubes of ice. For vegetables like tomatoes and asparagus, remove from the cooking water with a slotted spoon and cool completely for up to a minute in the cold water. For stocks, sauces or creams, pour the liquid into a bowl and set over the ice bath so that the cold water surrounds the base of the top bowl. Stir continuously until cool.

Peeling Tomatoes

Set a pot of water (large enough to submerge the number of tomatoes that need to be peeled) on the stove and bring to a boil. Meanwhile, cut each tomato. Turn the tomato over and make a light 'X' incision on the skin at the bottom. Prepare an ice bath. Place the tomatoes in the boiling water and let them cook for up to 20 seconds, depending on the size and ripeness of the tomato. (Smaller or riper tomatoes will require less time.) Remove with a slotted spoon and place in the cold water. When manageable, remove the tomatoes and peel, starting from the 'X' incision where the skin will peel nicely.

Re-hydrating Raisins or Dry Mushrooms

When using raisins or dried mushrooms, recipes will usually call to soak them in a particular liquid (often water or alcohol for dry fruits) to make them moist. Place the dried items in a small saucepan and barely cover with whichever liquid is called for. Gently reheat over a low heat for 5 minutes. Drain completely and set aside for use.

Splitting a Vanilla Bean

Run the tip of a small knife along the length of a vanilla bean to halve. Separate each half and press the blade of the knife against the cut side of the vanilla bean. In one motion, scrape the flesh of the inside and reserve. Repeat with the other half. Use both the shell and scraped flesh to flavour.

Nozioni Prime

BASICS

Maltagliati

Umbricelli

Cannelloni

Coxinhas

Bread

Delizia
al Limone

Balsamic Reduction Sauce
1 quantity

250 ml (8 fl oz) balsamic vinegar
125 ml (4 fl oz) red wine
125 ml (4 fl oz) port wine
4 black peppercorns

2 small shallots, peeled
1 bay leaf
2 inches of orange rind

––––––

Combine all the sauce ingredients in a small pot. Cook for 30 minutes over a low heat until the balsamic vinegar is like molasses. Pass through a sieve and discard the aromatics. Pour into a squeezable bottle and keep in the refrigerator for up to 1 month. Reheat by running warm water over the bottle or placing the bottle in a warm water bath for 5 minutes.

Basic Béchamel
1 quantity (250 ml or 8 fl oz)

250 ml (8 fl oz) whole milk
1 tablespoon butter

1 tablespoon flour
Salt, pepper and nutmeg to taste

––––––

Heat the milk in a small saucepan until it is just warm. In the meantime, melt the butter in a small saucepan over a medium heat. Add the flour to the melted butter and stir to combine with a whisk. When the roux is golden brown, add all the milk, whisking constantly so that it remains smooth. Season with salt, pepper and nutmeg. Pour into a separate container and cover with plastic wrap, making sure that the film touches the surface of the cream so that the surface does not develop a skin. Set aside for use.

Caper Parsley Sauce
1 quantity

2 tablespoons capers
3 tablespoons parsley

Extra virgin olive oil to cover

––––––

Wash and rinse the capers. Chop with the parsley and combine with the olive oil. Set aside until needed.

Cinnamon Sugar
1 quantity

4 tablespoons icing sugar

1 tablespoon ground cinnamon

––––––

Combine the sugar and cinnamon together in a bowl, then pass through a sieve. Keep in a cool, dry place until needed

Choux Pastry
1 quantity

312 ml (10½ fl oz) water
125 g (4½ oz) butter cut into cubes
Pinch of salt

160 g (5½ oz) Manitoba flour
3 eggs

———

Heat the water, butter and salt in a pot over a medium heat, melting the butter completely. As soon as the liquid comes to a boil, remove from the heat. Add the flour all at once and whisk well until combined. Return to the heat and continue to whisk for an additional 30 seconds, or until the dough pulls away from the sides and bottom of the pot. Remove from the heat and cool slightly. Mix in the eggs one at a time with a wooden spoon, incorporating completely after each addition. After mixing in the third egg, run a line through the centre of the dough. If the surrounding dough gradually fills in the line, the dough is ready.

Transfer into a piping bag with a 7 mm (⅜") tip and pipe out ½ tablespoon amounts onto a silicon mat or baking sheet. Lightly brush the top of each pastry with water and bake at Gas Mark 4/180°C/350°F for 20 minutes. Cool completely.

Caramel Lace
1 quantity

12 tablespoons sugar

———

Line a tray with parchment paper and spray with oil. Place the sugar in a heavy-bottomed saucepan and heat slowly so it begins to melt. When an even golden brown, remove from the heat and let stand to thicken slightly. Test the thickness by dipping a spoon into the caramel and waving the sugar back and forth over the paper. If the sugar comes out in long, fine threads that do not break easily, it is ready. Tilt the pan close to the tray and, with the spoon, run criss-crossing threads of caramel repeatedly over the entire parchment paper. Freeze for half an hour, then break into rough squares to beautifully decorate a dessert.

Chocolate Sauce
1 quantity

200 g (7 oz) bittersweet chocolate
150 ml (5¼ fl oz) double cream

———

Grate the chocolate and melt with the cream over a double boiler, mixing well. When smooth, remove from the heat and cool to room temperature. Pour into a squeezable bottle and refrigerate for up to 1 week. To reheat, place the bottle in a bowl filled with hot water, being careful that the water does not go inside the tip. This sauce may be drizzled over any number of desserts.

Four Cheese Sauce
1 quantity

84 g (3 oz) Taleggio
45 g (1½ oz) Emmenthal
45 g (1½ oz) Provolone
45 g (1½ oz) Pecorino di Pienza
150 ml (5 fl oz) milk
2 tablespoons single cream
1 tablespoon butter

―――――

Grate all the cheese and combine with the remaining ingredients over a double boiler. Melt over simmering water, gently mixing continuously with a wooden spoon. When the sauce is creamy, remove from the heat and keep covered until serving.

Ganache
1 quantity

380 g (13½ oz) 70% bittersweet chocolate
1½ tablespoons water
30 g (1 oz) sugar
125 ml (4 fl oz) double cream

―――――

Melt the chocolate over a double boiler. In a small pan, heat the water and sugar together until the sugar dissolves. Put in a separate bowl. Heat the cream to a boil and immediately pour into the syrup, whisking continuously. Add the melted chocolate to the mixture of syrup and cream and whisk quickly to incorporate well. The mixture will be bubbly. Let it rest for a few minutes until it is completely smooth and bubble-free (test by coating the back of a spoon for a shiny and smooth texture).

To glaze a cake, pour the warm glaze evenly over the cake, covering the surface. With a spatula, spread the glaze over the top and sides and refrigerate for 2 minutes to set. Slice and serve.

Ghee
1 quantity

Ghee is essentially clarified butter. Heat 225 g (8 oz) butter in a small stockpot and simmer over a low heat. Skim the milk solids as they come to the top until the butter is completely transparent and no more solids are present. Cool completely and keep in the fridge for up to 2 weeks.

Herb Yoghurt Sauce
1 quantity

150 ml (5 fl oz) double cream, lightly whipped
150 ml (5 fl oz) yoghurt
1 small garlic clove
1 tablespoon mixed herbs (chives, thyme, rosemary and basil), finely chopped
3 tablespoons extra virgin olive oil
Salt and black pepper
2 teaspoons lemon juice

———

Partly foam the double cream and mix in the remaining ingredients. Refrigerate until needed.

Lemon Strings Decoration
1 quantity

2 lemons
270 ml (9 fl oz) water

210 g (7 oz) sugar
1 tablespoon sugar

———

Shave the lemon rinds with a potato peeler along the length of the lemon. Set aside the fruit for later use. Cut the rind lengthwise in thin strings (julienne) with a sharp knife. Boil the water with the sugar until it melts. Keep 60 ml (2 fl oz) of this syrup aside. Bring half of the remaining syrup to a boil with the lemon rinds in it for half a minute. Drain the rinds through a sieve and repeat the procedure with the other half of the syrup (this process removes the bitterness of the rind). Pass the lemon strips through a sieve and return to the pot with the first 60 ml (2 fl oz) of syrup that you have previously put aside. Add 1 tablespoon of sugar. Bring to a boil, then reduce to a simmer and cook for 2 minutes. Remove the lemon strings from the liquid and set aside to cool until needed.

Mayonnaise
1 quantity (165 g or 5½ oz)

1 egg yolk
1 teaspoon mustard
150 ml (5 fl oz) vegetable oil
1 tablespoon lemon juice
Salt and pepper to taste

———

Mix the egg yolk and mustard together and add the oil in a slow, steady stream, whisking continuously. Add the remaining ingredients and set aside.

Olive Sauce

1 quantity

1 tablespoon chopped black olives
3 tablespoons olive oil
Salt to taste
½ garlic clove, smashed
A drop of Tabasco

———

Combine all the ingredients together and set aside until needed.

Orange Sauce

1 quantity

2 navel oranges
1 tablespoon cornflour
3 tablespoons white wine
1 teaspoon lemon juice
21 g (¾ oz) butter, at room temperature
Salt and white pepper to taste

———

Squeeze the oranges to get approximately 250 ml (8 fl oz) of juice. In a small saucepan, combine the orange juice, cornflour, white wine and lemon juice and cook over a medium heat until thickened, approximately 3 minutes. Remove from the heat and add the butter in teaspoon increments, continuously stirring until the sauce is smooth and creamy. Season to taste and keep warm.

Paneer

1 quantity (180 g or 6 oz)

1 litre (32 fl oz) milk
3 tablespoons lemon juice
2 level teaspoons salt

———

In a heavy-bottomed pot, heat the milk while stirring occasionally. As soon as the milk comes to a boil, add all the lemon juice and stir gently to curdle the milk. Remove from the heat when the mixture has separated between liquid and solid, and the liquid appears clear. (If the liquid remains cloudy, add a little more lemon juice.)

Line a colander with a large cheesecloth and pour the warm mixture into it. Close the cloth, press gently to squeeze out the liquid, and completely immerse in a bowl of water for 10 seconds. Take out, wring well and place back in the colander. Season with salt, weigh down with a heavy pot (adding water to the pot for extra weight) and leave for 4 hours, using a bowl to catch excess liquid. Refrigerate for up to 2 days.

Pepper Sauce
1 quantity

1 red bell pepper, washed
1 garlic clove, mashed
½ teaspoon balsamic vinegar
½ teaspoon red wine vinegar
2 tablespoons extra virgin olive oil
Salt, black pepper and white pepper to taste

_____

Place the pepper on a baking tray and cook at Gas Mark 4/180°C/350°F for 40 minutes or until the pepper has blackened. Remove the pepper from the oven and seal in a plastic bag until cool. Remove from the bag and peel. Cut off the stem, open and remove the seeds and any white flesh Purée the pepper in a blender with the garlic, vinegars, oil, salt and peppers. Cover the mixture and set aside.

Pesto
1 quantity

100 g (3½ oz) fresh basil leaves
2½ tablespoons pine nuts
2 garlic cloves
200 ml (7 fl oz) extra virgin olive oil
1 teaspoon salt
8 tablespoons grated Parmesan
4 tablespoons grated Pecorino Romano

_____

In a food processor, combine the basil, pine nuts, garlic, olive oil and salt and blend until fine. Pour into a small bowl and add the cheeses. Set aside until needed. If you decide to make a larger quantity to keep for the winter, leave out the cheese and garlic until the day of use. Keep frozen for up to 6 months and thaw completely before using.

Puff Pastry
1 quantity

500 g (18 oz) flour, plus more for dusting
175 ml (6 fl oz) cold water
1 teaspoon salt

1 teaspoon butter, at room temperature
500 g (18 oz) margarine, in flat block form

———

On a flat work surface or in a large bowl, combine the flour, cold water, salt and butter and work well with your hands. Knead until all the ingredients have been fully incorporated and are very even in texture. Wrap in plastic film, and refrigerate for 10 minutes. Dust a flat surface with flour (and continue to do so if the dough sticks) and open the dough to three times the width of the margarine block and 2 cm (¾") higher. Turn the dough so that the long side is facing you. Place the margarine in the centre and fold the dough like a tri-fold, first closing the left side then the right. Press the borders to encase completely. Rotate the block clockwise 90° and evenly pound the dough with a rolling pin to flatten. Roll out to a long strip 2 cm (¾") thick. Score the centre of the long strip crosswise and fold in both sides of the dough like a window pane so that the ends meet in the centre. Close again like you would a book. Wrap with plastic film and refrigerate for 10 minutes.

Roll the dough out into a long strip 5 mm (¼") thick. Close again like window panes, then like a book. Wrap in plastic film and refrigerate for another 10 minutes. Repeat four more times. Finally, portion the dough into four, wrap individually in plastic film, and freeze until needed. Remove from the freezer and set aside until at room temperature (approximately 2 hours) for use.

Saffron Parmesan Sauce
1 quantity

½ teaspoon saffron
50 g (1¾ oz) butter
125 ml (4 fl oz) milk
125 ml (4 fl oz) double cream

154 g (5½ oz) grated Parmesan
Black pepper to taste
Nutmeg

———

Soak the saffron threads in 225 ml (8 fl oz) of warm water for 1 hour.

Melt the butter in a pot and add the saffron and liquid. Add the milk and cream and heat until it starts to boil. Add the grated cheese and mix. Transfer to a double boiler and continue to cook, stirring continuously, until the sauce is very creamy, approximately 20 minutes. Season with black pepper and nutmeg and set aside until ready to serve.

Sage Butter Sauce
1 quantity

180 g (6½ oz) butter

6 sage leaves

———

Melt the butter over a low heat and add the sage. Keep over a medium heat for 3 minutes. Cool completely.

Seitan
1 quantity (800 g or 1 lb 12 oz)

Dough

1.4 kg (3 lb 2 oz) Manitoba flour
800 ml (26 fl oz) water

Cooking Liquid

3 litres (5¼ pints) water
1 tablespoon sea salt
100 ml (3 fl oz) white wine
100 ml (3 fl oz) soy sauce
1 carrot
1 onion, peeled
3 garlic cloves, peeled
1 celery stalk
1 sprig rosemary
1 sprig parsley

———

Combine the flour and water in a large bowl and work very well until smooth. Place the bowl in the sink. Squeeze and rinse the dough under running water continuously until the starchiness is washed away. This will be achieved once the rinsing water runs clear and the dough feels elastic. Drain over a colander and set aside. Prepare two large pots. In one pot, combine 2 litres (3½ pints) of water with 1 tablespoon of sea salt and bring to a simmer. In the other pot, combine the remaining cooking liquid ingredients and bring to a simmer as well. Remove the seitan from the colander and place on a flat work surface. Using your hands, roll the dough into a 10 cm (4") diameter log shape and slice into 1 cm (½") wide rounds. In batches, place the seitan in the pot of salted water. As soon as it comes to the surface, transfer with a slotted spoon into the second pot. Cook the seitan for an additional 20 minutes. Remove from the heat and allow the seitan to cool with its liquid. When cool, remove the seitan with a slotted spoon and delicately squeeze out the excess liquid. Refrigerate for up to 5 days.

Tartar Sauce
1 quantity

1 quantity Mayonnaise (see page 29)
2 green olives
2.5 cm (1") piece of carrot
1 gherkin
1 small shallot
1 small garlic clove
1 teaspoon chopped parsley

2.5 cm (1") celery leaves
2 capers
1 teaspoon mustard
Lemon juice to taste
2 drops of vinegar
Salt and black pepper to taste
1 tablespoon yoghurt

———

Blend all the ingredients together, except the yoghurt. Mix in the yoghurt and refrigerate.

Tomato Sauce
1 quantity (375 ml or 12½ fl oz)

800 g (26½ oz) canned peeled tomatoes
1 small carrot, peeled and halved lengthwise
1 small onion, peeled and halved
1 small celery stalk, cleaned and halved
1 sprig of parsley, rinsed

3 basil leaves, rinsed
2 garlic cloves, peeled and gently smashed
5 tablespoons extra virgin olive oil
1 teaspoon salt, or to taste

––––––

Pass the tomatoes through a food mill and discard the seeds. Combine the ingredients in a pot and cook over a medium-high heat. As soon as the sauce comes to a boil, reduce to a simmer and continue to cook for 20 minutes, uncovered, stirring occasionally. Taste for sweetness. If the sauce is too bitter, add some olive oil and a pinch of sodium bicarbonate (not sugar!) and simmer for an additional 5 minutes. Remove the aromatic vegetables with a slotted spoon and use the sauce as desired. If used solely as a sauce and not in addition to another recipe, this quantity will serve 4.

Truffle Sauce
1 quantity

3 tablespoons olive oil
1 garlic clove

1 tablespoon grated truffles
Pinch of salt

––––––

Heat the oil in a saucepan with the garlic. When the oil is hot and the garlic begins to brown, turn off the heat. Remove the garlic and add the truffles. Add a pinch of salt, stir and set aside.

Vegetable Stock
1.2 litres (2 pints)

2 litres (3½ pints) water
1 carrot, peeled and halved lengthwise
1 onion, peeled and quartered
1 celery stalk, halved
1 sprig fresh parsley

2 basil leaves
1 potato, peeled and quartered
1 courgette, quartered
1 garlic clove, peeled and gently smashed
Salt to taste

––––––

Combine all the ingredients in a large pot and bring to a boil. Reduce the heat, cover and simmer for 45 minutes. Strain through a fine sieve, cool and refrigerate for up to 3 days.

History

Truffles are rare and expensive as they are found underground and the collecting season is very short. They are a hypogenal fungi that can be found in north and central Italy. The most famous places for quality and quantity are Alba, Piedmont (especially for the more requested white truffles); Norcia, Umbria; and San Miniato, Toscana (for the black ones). With its strong and inebriating perfume and unique flavour, it reigns over all natural products. There is nothing more fascinating than truffles.

A little more history

Since 3000 BC, Babylonian times, there are records of the use of an ingredient similar to truffles. In the second century BC, Teofrasto di Ereso, one of the Aristotelian students studying botany, discussed truffles in his 'Historia Plantarum'. According to the Greek philosopher, the fungus was reaching the peak of its taste thanks to a combination of rain and lightning. Galen, the father of systematic medicine in the second century BC, reported its very nutritious qualities and its power to raise spirits. The mysterious fungus became an aphrodisiac believed to bestow pleasure.

In the Roman Empire, truffles were dedicated to Venus, the goddess of love. Doctors gave them to many patients for impotence, the first case of 'Viagra'. In the first century AD, Apicio, a famous gourmet from one of the oldest 'Patrizi' families of ancient Rome, talked about the royal quality of truffles in meals, elevating the fungus to a noble status.

In medieval times, the appreciation ended. Truffles were considered to be dangerous since consumers were suddenly thought to have a demonic nature. For a time, truffles nearly disappeared completely, only to reappear during the time of the Comuni e della Signorie, a few centuries later. They were raised again to a level of high demand, and the elite made a point of having truffles on their tables. Even Francesco Petrarca, the famous poet, composed verses about the fungus.

In this period, two of the most royal types of truffles were discovered: Il Tuber Magnatum and Il Tuber Melanosporum. Until this period, people had been satisfied with poorer quality.

In the Renaissance, however, truffles reached their greatest glory, generating a kind of addiction: In any respectable banquet, truffles had to be present. In this period, the best chefs, the Masters of Cuisine (those of the nobility), were trying hard to create new recipes to offer their illustrious guests, incorporating the fungus in their dishes and even giving it as a prestigious gift.

Truffles, naturally, could not be missing among the many different products that Caterina de Medici took with her to France. She contributed to the widespread use of them when she went to marry Enrico II.

In the 1800s, truffles were the symbol of nobility and wealth. Many kings and emperors, Napoleon included, were excited by the taste of the fungus. Even during the final lunch of the Congress of Vienna (dated 1815), where the greatest politicians and state leaders of the world gathered, truffles were present.

Truffle growing

Tartufaie is the area where truffles are found naturally. Unfortunately these places are becoming more scarce and/or decreasing in size because of atmospheric situations.

For many years, people have been practising artificial cultivation, with some results. As truffles are symbiotic with the roots of oak and hazelnut, these trees are planted with truffle spores inoculated in them. Truffles get water and salts from the earth to the plants while the plants give refined carbohydrates to the truffles.

The main competitors for man, in finding truffles, are generally wild boars, which are very common in the areas of production. They simply love the fungus and concrete fences have been made around 'tartufaie' to prevent boars digging them up.

Note on saffron

Originally, saffron was from Asia Minor. It has been used in dyes, medicines and cosmetics, as well as in cooking. Well known from the Nile River region, saffron was also renowned among the Greeks, as they used it in drawings on the walls of the palace in Knossus. In Italy, since the thirteenth century, this plant has been widely used to dye linen, wool and silk, and used as a paint. Il Perugino, Pietro Vannucci, the master of Raffael, took the flowers, extracted the colour and used it for his famous paintings and frescos. He encouraged the cultivation of the plant in the area of Lake Trasimeno in Umbria. Spanish saffron became more affordable than the local expensive Umbrian one. After the Rennaissance it almost stopped being produced commercially and almost disappeared in this area.

In his perfectly tailored cream-coloured Valentino suit and polished chocolate brown Armani loafers, forty-four year old Alberto Musacchio is the archetype of classic Italian style as he ambles from one table to another in his restaurant. From the dining room, one can hear the roars of laughter from guests reacting to one of his many stories while he charms them with his boyish smile.

With a slim 6'1" frame and salt and pepper hair, he has a sophisticated manner about him and is as strict with his own appearance as he is with the quality of food at his restaurant. To imagine the elegance of Alberto as having been any less or different than it is today is an absurd notion, as even he would allow.

Personal archive picture

In actuality, the Alberto Musacchio of 1979 would vary greatly from today's version.

During the transition between the experimental seventies and decadent eighties, Perugia became the international student capital of Italy. The city's university offered a three-month Italian language programme to follow further studies in other cities like Rome, Florence and Milan. It was in this city that nineteen-year-old fair-skinned Alberto

decided to study philosophy at the university. After travelling cross-country in the United States with only 300 dollars in his pocket, he had long lost the *naïveté* of the young teenager he once was, while growing a full head of hair down to his shoulders in the process. He was eager to enjoy everything the world had to offer him, while capitalizing on his greatest strength: his business-savvy entrepreneurial foresight.

Perugia had made a quick change from quiet medieval city to a bustling and trendy university town overnight. With young students pouring in and sharing wild antics with one another, the local establishments had hardly a fair opportunity to catch up, a detail Alberto picked up right away. His best memories from the States were of hanging out in small pubs and lounges, where anything from quiet conversations to raucous gatherings were the norm, and he found that it was exactly what Perugia was lacking. There were small cafés that served coffee and closed early, or discotheques for all-night dancing, but nowhere for people to go to hang out, listen to good music, have a few drinks and relax.

In the historical centre of the city was a small dive recognized for small-time drug laundering, macrobiotic food and poor business. In Alberto's eyes, it was a goldmine. With the financial backing of his parents, Alberto, his older brother Gianni and his classmate Fedele, bought the bar from the eager-to-sell owners and took it upon themselves to shape the place into their dream pub.

They named their pub 'Califfo' after a book called '*Il Califfo dell'Hashish*' by the French author Gerald de Nerval. The book, written in 1851, spread through the underground of the free-thinking and liberal-minded youth and rapidly gathered a cult following in the seventies. It inspired Alberto and his partners and made their pub recognizable by the crowd they wanted to attract. One of their friends created a stunning mosaic made of stained glass and

'ghironda', or hurdy gurdy, through the streets of the city, attracting an audience and eventually leading them to Califfo on opening night. That evening, Alberto, Gianni, and Fedele served well over 200 people, marking the beginning of a lucrative and exciting journey.

The next seven years were dedicated to living the high life. Alberto and his partners, in their early twenties, thrived off this lifestyle, working at the pub until the early morning hours, partying with friends and watching the sunrise after closing, then passing out until the afternoon before heading back to work. They enjoyed the throng of students who came in waves from all parts of the world, leaving after the three-month programme ended to be replaced by a new group of people.

Alberto, Gianni, and Fedele all took Califfo very seriously but no one had any aspirations of making the relaxed pub into an upmarket restaurant. Their profit came from beverage sales and various vegetarian sandwiches.

copper linings for the entrance of the pub, replicating the cover of the book. The gloriously attired sultan is a beautiful piece of artwork that still remains in the city to this day.

It was around this time that Alberto, Gianni and Fedele decided to wear white, and only white, as a symbol of purity and cleanliness. It was an outrageous, yet distinctively cool, decision that set them apart and made them known throughout the city for several years.

From the start, Califfo was a huge success. It was the perfect place at the perfect time, attracting waves of international students from the opening day. Alberto, Gianni and Fedele had put up flyers and posters around the city and in the halls of the university to advertise its grand opening, but it was actually a hired street performer who brought in the largest crowd. Alberto and his partners paid a musician to play a

During the first year of business, one chef began to frequent the pub and seized an opportunity to work in the kitchen. He began to help at no cost to Alberto and his partners, first preparing sandwiches and later more involved vegetarian dishes.

Seeing potential, the partners hired him and began to pay him for the work that he was doing. Almost immediately, the chef began to neglect his responsibilities and started working less and less. The chef lasted six months before Alberto fired him for stealing money from the cash registers, and silently for also trying to seduce his girlfriend. It was only a few months later when Akira took over the kitchen, at which point the culinary element took off.

Students loved going to Califfo because the ambience was young and vibrant. Street artists would be given free food and lodgings in the apartment upstairs when they came to perform, so there were always musicians, magicians and mime artists performing on a small stage in the pub. Alberto and his partners were more than the owners, they were friends and entertainers. Under the guise of magic tricks, Alberto would flirt with the girls who came into the bar night after night. Patrons loved it when Alberto rode his unicycle over to their tables to deliver their drinks, adding to the wacky and fantastic feel of the pub. On one cool November evening in 1982, business was as usual. A group of architecture students had just arrived from Brazil and, naturally, found their way to Califfo. Alberto, with his back to the entrance, had been chatting with some people sitting at the bar when he felt and heard the front door swing open. Simultaneously, every man in the pub went wide-eyed and slackjawed, and instinct told Alberto that someone beautiful had just walked into his bar. Turning his head, he joined the throng of mesmerized men when he saw Malu, an amazon of a woman with a mane of curly golden hair, tanned skin against high cheekbones and the longest legs he had ever seen in his life. She was wearing jeans and a colourful tank top and had an unassuming, open air about her that brought life into his pub.

When Malu approached him at the bar to order a drink, he pulled out all the stops and performed a foolproof magic trick that always, always impressed the girls. On Malu, the trick did not work and Alberto failed miserably. Seeing that he was embarrassed, she gave him a warm smile and went back to her table with her drink. Alberto noticed that she sat down next to one particularly handsome man and, feeling his defeat, went back to work. The following day, when the same gentleman showed up at the bar with one of Perugia's most recognized homosexuals, Alberto saw his window of opportunity re-open and leapt through it.

For the next few days, he couldn't help but keep one eye out for her whenever he walked around the city. He would step into a bar and take a quick scan to see if she was there. He would sit on the steps in the main plaza with a slice of pizza and casually look around for her. Some days he was lucky and managed to get a glimpse of her. Other days he would not. Malu began frequenting his pub and slowly began to build a relationship with her future husband. Within a few weeks, they were dating. Alberto was beside himself and Malu, on her side, was taken in by this skinny man with long hair and white clothes. He was funny and intelligent, but what captured her was his unspoken and innate desire for something inexplicably spiritual.

They had been seeing each other for nearly two weeks when he had a day off and wanted to spend it with her. While she wanted to go to Florence for the day with a friend, he wanted her to stay in the city and spend the day with him. Both were stubborn, fiery individuals. Inadvertently attracting the attention of nearby bricklayers, they broke out into a fierce

argument. The fight was less about how they were going to spend the day and more about who was going to listen to whom. In the end, Malu went to Florence and Alberto spent his day alone. It poured the entire day and, while both felt that they were justified in some way, neither really knew what they had really won.

Three months later, when Malu had finished her language programme in Perugia, she headed to Rome for six months to study architectural restoration and continued to visit Alberto in Perugia. He, in turn, spent his days off in Rome with her. Their strong personalities clashed numerous times and they fought constantly over small things, but by the time she was finished in Rome and was to leave for Brazil, she had decided to stay in Italy, in Perugia, to be with Alberto.

Aside from Masa, the Japanese sous chef, Akira allowed no other individual in the kitchen. He was a proud man and lived for his work, and for anyone to come in and take away any of his responsibilities was an insult. Although Akira liked Malu and knew that she was dating his boss, her presence in the kitchen, as anyone else's, would not be tolerated.

On one particularly busy night, more people than usual were placing orders and, with Masa off, Akira was swamped. As the tickets piled in, dirty pans and dishes remained stacked in the sink and Akira was up to his neck in work. Without a word, Malu appeared, washed and dried all the dishes, and left as silently as she had come in. Akira, upon noticing this act, adored her instantly. Over the next few years, he became her teacher and mentor in the kitchen. All the while, he felt and acted like a schoolboy whenever she stepped into the room.

The vigorous years of owning Califfo wore down the owners. They were exhausted from working such long hours late into the evening and were no longer the flamboyant, pleasure seeking youths they once were. All three had grown into serious, colour-wearing

individuals who were anxious to embark on the next chapter in their lives. Six months after Akira left and Masa took his place, Masa lost one leg in a serious motorcycle accident. Shortly after, Alberto and his partners decided to move on.

Seven years after the opening of Califfo, Alberto, Gianni, and Fedele sold their beloved pub to a group of wealthy footballers. Without the original owners, the pub lost its charm and appeal and, over the next 20 years, passed through several hands. Remarkably, guests continue to come to Montali and speak of this fantastic pub they hung out at while studying in Perugia back in the early eighties. Their mouths open in surprise when they find out that Alberto was the original owner. Slowly, their eyes give them away as they realize that the bohemian, fair-skinned, long-haired boy behind the renowned bar is now the distinguished gentleman sitting before them.

THE BRAZILIAN FLOWER

If Giuseppe Sarti had lived to see Malu grow into a woman, his heart would have been full of pride for his granddaughter. Even more than his own children, she shared her grandfather's fierce commitment to his beliefs, his affection that he generously poured over his family and, in particular, his passion for food and cooking.

Born and raised in Modena, he met and married a young girl from Rimini and together they emigrated to San Paolo, Brazil, at the turn of the 19th century. He was proud of his heritage and maintained a strong Italian-blooded household, raising his children on tales of old Italian folklore, memories of the stunning landscape and architecture and traditional food, song and dance. He started earning money by selling food in the village and gradually expanded his business.

Eventually, he had money to build a house that was large enough for his entire extended family to come together to sing, dance and eat.

Giuseppe died when Malu was only two years old, but her youth was full of countless stories he had passed down. From an early age, she was fascinated by the rich Italian history and culture, the pictures she had seen of historical structures and monuments, and the considerable differences between each region. She fell in love with the imagery of the rustic lifestyle and stories of festivals celebrating the fruits of the earth.

Malu was a vivacious and energetic child who loved school, music and sports. While she enjoyed the dishes her mother expertly prepared, she drank a lot of fluids but never ate much. She was eleven years old when her height began to soar at an alarming rate and her mother, seeing her skinny daughter stretching out, grew nervous. After seeing a doctor, Malu was no longer allowed to enjoy sports like swimming and running for fear that they encouraged her growth spurt.

Nevertheless, she continued to grow well into her mid-twenties.

When she was 16, she was still very skinny with more arms and legs than she knew what to do with, but she also began to suffer intense migraines and stomach cramps. Slowly, she discovered that on days when she happened to not eat meat, she felt better and had more energy.

Over the course of three years, Malu slowly weaned herself off meat until she completely avoided it. A few years later, after witnessing a bucket full of live lobsters being thrown into a steaming pot and cooked to their death, she gave up seafood as well.

Malu developed her love of cooking early on from her mother, often taking her place in the kitchen to cook for her brother and sister. She followed recipes and experimented on her own. Sometimes, the outcome was incredible. Other times, it was a complete disaster. Although Malu loved tasting new and interesting flavours, she took the greatest pleasure in the purity of the simplest dishes, from roasted potatoes to pastel, a Brazilian pizza-like dough stuffed with cheese and deep-fried.

After studying architecture for a number of years, 26-year-old Malu found out about a scholarship being offered by the Italian government that would send Brazilian architecture graduates to study in Italy. Following a vigorous application process, Malu was awarded one of the ten coveted scholarships. She had just started studying the Italian language and was ahead of the rest of her classmates by the time they all arrived in Perugia.

As a shock to no one, both Italians and Brazilians are meat lovers. Pork, beef, lamb and veal are featured in most dishes, used to flavour sauces, and stuffed inside dumplings, vegetables and even other cuts of meat. Despite the similarity in the two diets, Malu found it difficult to avoid eating meat when she first arrived in Italy. Slowly, she happened upon cafés in the centre of the city that offered vegetarian entrées. She had always liked beans, nuts and cheeses and fell in love with Italy for the wealth of all three in the cuisine. She discovered rustic dishes like lentil soups and pasta e fagioli, pasta with fresh beans, traditionally served all over southern Italy.

One of her friends had told her about a popular vegetarian pub called Califfo in the heart of the city by the university. There were few places for students to congregate, have drinks and meet other international students, and the atmosphere that Califfo promised was exactly what Malu and her friends sought.

Malu stepped into Califfo with a group of students and discovered a lively pub with great music and a spirited staff. At the bar, she noticed a tall and skinny young man wearing white jeans and a white short-sleeved shirt. Later, when he made his way over to her table, she became aware of his big, sparkling eyes and long wavy hair. She was immediately taken by the fresh energy and exuberant charm that he exuded and the two began speaking as if they were old

friends. Later in the night, only Malu, an intimate group of her friends, Alberto, Gianni and Fedele remained in the pub. They spoke together in a mixture of Italian, English and Portuguese and somehow communicated perfectly with one another. Malu and Alberto bounced off each other the entire night, making witty comments while discovering how similar they both were. Malu was impressed by how cosmopolitan Alberto and his friends appeared to be and revelled in the open atmosphere of the late night. She was surprised to hear that Alberto was five years younger than she was because, although he had a very young energy about him, he was mature beyond his years and already had clear ideas of what he wanted from life.

Malu and her friends spent the next three days exploring the rest of Perugia's nightlife before finally going back to Califfo. Every once in a while, she would walk with some friends in the city and see Alberto walking up the same road, his secretive smile teasing her. They soon began dating and quickly grew close. Alberto adored her and loved being in her company, wanting to spend every waking moment with her. Malu felt the same way, but still refrained from becoming serious with anyone she would have to leave in a number of months. Malu had always been an independent person and insisted on spending time on her own to study or travel, a mindset that spurred many of their arguments.

One fight in particular presented the first fork in the road of their relationship. She and a friend had decided to visit Florence on the same day that Alberto had his day off. He wanted her to stay with him and she insisted on going with her friend. Fuming from the argument that followed, she went back to her dorm room that she shared with other students. A few hours later, she sat on the stairwell with her face resting on her hands when she heard someone come up behind her.

"I have a present for you," Alberto said quietly. He held out an exquisite lapis lazuli necklace before her. Before placing it around her neck, he paused. "So, you'll stay?"

Malu's eyes darkened and a bitter argument erupted instantly. "Do you think you can come in here and buy my time? Is that it? You show up here with expensive jewellery and expect me to do whatever you want?"

The row quickly escalated into a shouting match and drew the attention of anyone within hearing range. Malu, who was still learning Italian, found the words pouring out of her and Alberto fought back matching every ounce of her anger with his own.

Alberto grabbed Malu's hand, thrust the necklace into her palm and said, "You can keep the necklace!" Malu watched as he stormed down the stairs in his white pants and white high tops and opened the door at the base of the steps. He stepped out, threw one more look at her, and dramatically slammed the door. Malu seethed. His stubbornness was so Italian and she was determined to stand her ground.

The next day, she went to Florence with her friend where it rained non-stop the entire time.

She was wet, cold, and depressed, blaming Alberto for the miserable weather.

She and her friend, both soaked, took the bus from Florence back to the centre of Perugia. They were dropped off at the bus station and headed down the main street when she saw Alberto walking towards her. He knew which bus she had taken home and wanted to meet her when she stepped off. Her heart warmed when she saw his guilty expression until the second he opened his mouth with a smirk and asked, "So, how was the weather?"

Malu opened her mouth, a quick retort on the tip of her tongue, but she had had a long day and was tired. "Let's go get coffee," was all she said and they walked, hand in hand, to a nearby café.

After Malu's Italian language course ended, she left Perugia to complete her programme studies in Rome. Despite the distance between Rome and Perugia, Malu and Alberto saw each other regularly. She remained devoted to her programme and career and she yearned to travel the world with no constraints. She was able to envision an exciting lifestyle with this young and vibrant man who shared her eagerness to experience new thrilling adventures. Over the following months their relationship continued to grow and, although they still fought constantly, Malu and Alberto thrived in each other's company.

Time and time again, she felt torn in her feelings for him. She saw a life with him, but one in which she would have to compromise the dreams she had held onto for so many years. It was towards the end of her programme, during a trip to Istanbul with Alberto, when Malu finally decided that she would hold off returning to Brazil to stay in Perugia with him.

Alberto involved Malu in Califfo's activities over the following years and she became a faithful presence in the bar. She loved the unique characteristics that the three owners brought to the business. Alberto was always full of energy, always inventive and excited to take on new challenges. Gianni was the mystic, a sociologist turned-pub owner with undoubtable artistic tendencies. Fedele was the calming, grounded force that relaxed both the workers and the high-energy clientele. With Akira and Masa, the air was filled with a thick, yet delicate creative energy. After a busy night, the six of them would stay up until four in the morning to plan for the following day, share ideas and experiment with new flavours. It was a time in their lives when they were all brimming with excitement over the endless possibilities the world had to offer. Years later, Malu would recall the great meeting of minds, and much of who she became was affected by her experiences at Califfo.

Years later, Malu and Alberto married and settled in the Umbrian countryside. Stone by stone, they built the Country House Montali. They built their dream from the ground up, supported only by each other and the innate desire they shared to create something different and wonderful. Montali, they decided, would not be another piece of property with rooms and pre-cooked, unexceptional food. It was to be a haven for guests from around the world, providing an incredible, fulfilling experience in both the serenity of the countryside and in the breaking of bread with others who shared this desire.

For Malu, being the provider of a style of food that redefines vegetarianism, being able to introduce others to unexpectedly and incredibly melded flavours and ingredients is the most rewarding element of Montali. Vegetarians come on holiday and need not worry about what they are eating, while non-vegetarians are awestruck at how delectable and satisfying meatless food can be.

Whenever guests catch her in the kitchen after an exceptional dinner and say, "Malu, that was the most wonderful meal I have ever had in my life," she always, always gets goose bumps. It is something she has heard time and time again throughout the years and yet it still affects her as

if she is being told for the first time. It is her unique and humble ability to continue to take such pleasure in daily occurrences. She never ceases to amaze those around her when she sits down in the morning with her breakfast and sighs with delight while biting into a croissant, the same croissant she has had every day for so many years.

A few years ago, Malu's Brazilian aunt arrived at Montali on her first visit. While she fell in love with everything from the tranquillity of the olive grove to the delicious and fulfilling meals that Malu prepared, she was most astonished by how similar Montali was to Guiseppe Sarti's village home so many years ago. The familiarity and warmth of his house created a contented setting for all his guests to enjoy while he took pleasure in planning and preparing nourishing foods for them. So much of who he was and what he strived for had somehow remarkably been revived by a granddaughter who had never known him. For most, it is a beautiful coincidence. For Malu, it tells her she is really home.

Prima Colazione

BREAKFAST

CIAMBELLA

This traditional chocolate and yoghurt swirl cake is a favourite among children and adults alike at the Country House Montali. Enjoy with a glass of cold milk or a steaming cup of café latte.

Serves 10 Ⓔ *15 minutes & 35 minutes baking & cooling time*

INGREDIENTS

Butter and flour for dusting

3 eggs

180 g (6½ oz) sugar

Pinch of salt

120 ml (4 fl oz) sunflower oil

112 ml (4 fl oz) plain yoghurt

260 g (9¼ oz) Italian '00' flour

1½ teaspoons baking powder

Zest of 1 lemon

60 g (2 oz) miniature chocolate chips

1 tablespoon cocoa powder

———

Preheat the oven to Gas Mark 4/175°C/350°F. Butter and flour a 23 cm (9") spring-form cake tin. In a medium-sized bowl, beat eggs with the sugar and salt until the mixture is pale and frothy. Slowly add oil into the batter, stirring continuously. Add the yoghurt, sift in the flour and baking powder and then add the lemon zest, mixing well after each addition. Fold in the chocolate chips. Pour two-thirds of the batter into the cake tin. Sift and fold in the cocoa powder into the remaining batter and pour evenly over the light batter. Bake for 35 minutes. Remove from the heat and cool. Ciambella may be served warm or at room temperature.

MUESLI

This tasty recipe is one of the best ways to nourish your body in the morning. Rich in fibre from the cereal and full of vitamins from the fruit, it has the benefit of fresh yoghurt as well.

Serves 6 Ⓔ *20 minutes*

INGREDIENTS

130 g (4½ oz) oats

1½ tablespoons coconut flakes

3 tablespoons almonds, toasted and chopped

4 tablespoons raisins, soaked in hot water and drained

1 apple, peeled, cored and cubed

1 pear, peeled, cored and cubed

1 banana, peeled and cubed

½ tablespoon coconut syrup

300 ml (10 oz) yoghurt

Mosto Cotto (see page 17), honey or maple syrup for drizzling

Poppy seeds

———

In a dry, non-stick pan, toast the oats until golden brown. Add the coconut flakes and toast for an additional 30 seconds. Remove from the heat and place in a bowl. Toss with the almonds, raisins and fruit and add the coconut syrup. Divide into small bowls, drizzle with yoghurt and Mosto Cotto and sprinkle with poppy seeds.

TORTA di MAIS

When visiting new babies in the neighborhood, Malu's mother would bake the new mother this delightful corn and aniseed cake. The corn gives a healthy boost of energy while the aniseed provides essential nutrients that the mother can pass along to her infant. Aside from the health benefits, the subtle sweetness and the appealing texture of corn blend deliciously, especially when complemented by tea or a cappuccino.

Serves 12 Ⓔ *35 minutes & 45 minutes baking & cooling time*

INGREDIENTS

300 g (11 oz) cornmeal
400 g (14½ oz) sugar
500 ml (16 fl oz) milk
100 ml (3¼ fl oz) vegetable oil
1 tablespoon butter
4 eggs, separated
1 tablespoon aniseed
1 tablespoon baking powder
1 teaspoon vanilla extract
Pinch of salt
Icing sugar, for dusting

―――――

Butter a 25 x 38 cm (10 x 15") baking tin, flour the sides and line the bottom with parchment paper.

Combine the cornmeal, sugar, milk, oil and butter in a saucepan and whisk continuously over a medium heat. After about 10 minutes the mixture should start to pull away from the pot. Continue to cook for an additional 3 minutes, then remove from the heat and cool completely.

Lightly beat the egg yolks and add to the cooled batter with the aniseed, sifted baking powder and vanilla. Beat well to incorporate air.

In a separate bowl, beat the egg whites with the salt to stiff peaks. Gently fold a third of the egg whites into the batter until fully incorporated before adding the remaining egg whites.

Pour the batter into the pan and spread evenly with a spatula. Bake at Gas Mark 4/180°C/350° for 45 minutes or until a toothpick, when inserted, comes out clean. Cool in the pan before removing. Dust the surface with icing sugar and serve.

ALUA

This widely-known Indian dish is prepared after a religious fast. Here you'll find it with a fancy Montali variation of coconut syrup, roasted nuts and fresh fruit.

Serves 5   (M)   *20 minutes*

INGREDIENTS

500 ml (16 fl oz) milk

3 whole cardamom seeds

1 tablespoon butter

100 g (3½ oz) semolina

1 tablespoon coconut flakes

225 g (½ lb) mixed fruit: bananas, pears, apples, peaches, etc., cut into 1 cm (½") cubes

1 tablespoon coconut syrup

2 tablespoons raisins, soaked in hot water and drained

3 tablespoons almonds, toasted and chopped

Poppy seeds

Mosto Cotto (see page 17), honey or maple syrup

––––––

Heat the milk in a saucepan. Grind the cardamom seeds in a mortar and pestle, removing the skins and crushing the pods. Melt the butter in a medium-sized pot and add the ground cardamom to infuse for ½ minute. Roast the semolina in the infused butter until the semolina begins to brown. Add the coconut flakes and continue to cook for 30 seconds.

Turn off the heat and carefully add the hot milk all at once, whisking constantly. Return to the heat and continue to cook, stirring, until the mixture is no longer runny. Stir in the fruit, coconut syrup, raisins and almonds. Top with a sprinkle of poppy seeds and a drizzle of Mosto Cotto.

FRUTTA FRITTA

Sliced fruit dipped in a light batter and delicately fried to golden perfection. Try it with various fruits other than just apples, bananas, peaches and pears.

Serves 8 Ⓜ *15 minutes & 10 minutes for resting batter*

BATTER

2 eggs
8 tablespoons '00' flour
1½ teaspoons baking powder
2 tablespoons cornflour
140 ml (4½ fl oz) milk
60 ml (2 fl oz) cognac
2 drops of vanilla essence

———

Mix all ingredients until smooth and rest for 10 minutes.

FRUIT

Vegetable oil, for deep frying
4 bananas, peeled and halved lengthwise
2 apples, peeled, cored and sliced horizontally, 5 mm (¼") thick
3 peaches, cored and sliced
3 pears, cut into wedges
Cinnamon Sugar (see page 26)

———

Heat the oil in a large pot. Dip the fruit in the batter to coat completely and deep fry in batches. Remove the fruit individually with a slotted spoon when golden brown all around. Sprinkle the Cinnamon Sugar over the top and serve hot.

CRESPELLE FARCITE con FRUTTA e MIELE

Light, golden pancakes stuffed with fruit and honey.

Serves 4 Ⓔ *15 minutes & 10 minutes for resting batter*

CRÊPES

7 tablespoons Italian '00' flour
½ teaspoon baking powder
5 tablespoons cognac
150 ml (5 fl oz) milk
2 drops of vanilla extract

———

Whisk the batter ingredients together in a bowl and rest for 10 minutes. Heat and lightly butter a non-stick pan over medium-high heat. Remove the pan from the heat, ladle a spoonful of batter into the pan and gently swirl to coat the surface. Place back on the heat and cook until one side is golden brown. Flip to cook the other side. Slide the crêpe onto a plate and repeat with the remaining batter.

FILLING

1 apple, cored and thinly sliced
1 pear, cored and thinly sliced
1 banana, thinly sliced

ASSEMBLY

Honey, for drizzling
Mosto Cotto (see page 17), honey or maple syrup
Icing sugar, for dusting

———

Cover one-quarter of each crêpe with fruit. Fold in half, then in quarters. Insert more fruit into the upper quarter. Drizzle over honey and Mosto Cotto, dust with icing sugar and serve.

"This," the wealthy miller said pleasantly while accepting Malu and Alberto's money, "is like a packet of cigarettes to me." One of the few remaining survivors of the original six owners, the miller had been trying to sell his unused mountain top property for so many years that the buying price had dropped to, in his mind, pocket change. What was once beautiful hunting territory and cultivated soil 50 years earlier had turned into rocky jungle terrain that sat in close proximity to the medieval Castello di Montali. Contrary to the miller's view, the 25-acre land held a world of dreams for young Malu and Alberto.

After years of splitting time between Califfo and various trips to India, Malu and Alberto had decided that the time had come to buy land of their own and settle down. They were tired of city life and longed for peace in the countryside where they could grow organic foods and continue self-growth. They dreamed of a place where sunlight would be unobstructed by tall buildings, trees or even hills.

With his share of money after selling Califfo, in addition to a small sum he had inherited, Alberto began looking with Malu for their new home. For eight months, they exhausted themselves driving all over the country in their relentless search. Each potential acquisition came with numerous problems. If the price was good, the soil was ruined. If the land was nice, electricity would be next to impossible to obtain. If everything else was perfect, there was still the issue of running water being unavailable. Every place they had emotionally invested in had ultimately disappointed them.

In the most casual of circumstances, Alberto voiced his frustrations to the landlord of his small apartment, who, after hearing what they were searching for, told Alberto of a secluded and uninhabited piece of property on top of a mountain that had been on the market for 15 years. With nothing to lose, Alberto, Malu and their landlord drove to the top of the road-less mountain to have a look at this undesired land. What was one man's trash was another man's treasure as they fell in love instantly. The two small buildings in the centre were covered in vines and the earth had obviously been neglected, but the panorama was endless, the air was clean and fresh running water was plentiful. It was perfect.

They sought the owner immediately, who was overjoyed at the prospect of finally selling off his land and being able to be the source of happiness to such a romantically idealistic couple. Malu and Alberto took their ownership papers and drove straight back to their new home. With a view as far as Assisi, Malu was overwhelmed with joy. As she walked next to her husband, she grasped his hand and jumped in the air. "All this...this is our land! Can you imagine?" she said breathlessly. Alberto smiled at his wife from the corner of his mouth and replied, "No need to get so emotional. It's just land." But her excitement was infectious.

They spent the first few days giving the property a thorough assessment. Although Malu was an architect by profession, neither she nor her husband had had experience with tilling soil, cultivation or manual construction of buildings. They discovered that the two buildings on the property were in much worse condition than they had first believed. The roof of the garage was completely caved in, as was half of the roof over the main house. The antique tiles, in great demand across the country, had been stolen from the roof years before, and the fireplace refused to function properly, emitting smoke but no flames or heat. Random plant-life was growing inside the abandoned home and plumbing was nonexistent.

A Sicilian agronomist came to inspect the soil to determine its usability. After spending hours going over every inch, he sat Alberto and Malu down. "Well, this is truly a lovely panorama you have bought here. However, it's dangerously close to desertification. Turning this land into something is going to be next to impossible, but with a lot of work I'm sure you can plant an olive grove." It was the only thing they needed to hear before getting started.

Cleaning the soil was the first priority. At the hardware store they bought a few small ploughs and gloves to start with, but after a few hours of accomplishing nothing, they looked at each other and said, "We're going to need a bigger plough." Soon, they realized larger ploughs were not the solution. They were going to have to call in a tractor-driven plough. The soil was packed with bulky rocks that they had to carry, one by one, to a large pile for later use. What few olive trees there were, were crowded by thorny bushes and weeds. When the shrubbery was hacked away with machetes, branches sprang back unpredictably like elastic, viciously whacking the offender. Their faces and arms were soon covered in cuts and bruises.

Cultivating the soil was an arduous task that lasted years. It was not uncommon for Malu or Alberto to plop down under one of the hundreds of olive trees they were planting and weep out of frustration, exhaustion and loss of hope. The less distressed one would assume the reassuring role, pushing the other in their belief towards accomplishing their dream. Often the only words were, "Remember India? There's nothing we can't do."

Four winters in a row were spent in the brutal cold. There was no heating during those years and as the fireplace was not functional, keeping warm on a mountaintop was impossible. The roof was the first segment of the buildings to be fixed and Malu continuously transported cement that she had just hand-mixed to her husband and another bricklayer. Only much later did they decide to buy a machine-operated cement mixer. Both Malu and Alberto became involved in every facet of the building process. Countless mistakes significantly lengthened the building process and added to their frustration. The garage-turned-meditation room was rebuilt twice while the entire plumbing system had to be placed. Alberto discovered a talent for bricklaying and, by watching carefully, learned the tricks of the old professional bricklayer who was helping them. They contracted a man to lay the road as barely a path had existed before.

After a few years, enough of their home was built for them to open the doors to the public as a place for spiritual gathering. Malu would feed the groups that came to their home to experience music therapy or learn about meditation. Built with the idea of a retreat centre in mind, Malu and Alberto believed that donations would sustain their humble venture and had no specific billing process. It was during this time that Alberto received a letter from his mother, Wanda. She was elderly, but independent, strong and visionary. Not only did Wanda believe in what her son and his wife were creating, she also knew she could help them in many ways. She could have lived with her eldest son, Gigi, in his estate in Piedmont, or comfortably with Gianni in Assisi, but she chose to help Alberto and Malu. Malu was thrilled at the idea of her mother-in-law coming to live with them. An instant bond had developed between them the moment they met years earlier and Wanda became like a second

Photo courtesy of Claudio 'the Barber'

mother to Malu, whose own mother had passed away. Alberto, on the other hand, felt divided. His mother, he knew, would be an enormous help, particularly now when Malu was expecting their first child. On the other hand, his was still a harsh life that he could not ask anyone else to share, especially his own mother. Wanda assured her son that she did not mind that there was no heating, and that helping them would give her a strong sense of purpose. Despite his disinclination, Alberto welcomed his mother.

Wanda immediately became a strong source of encouragement for her son and daughter-in law. She was an elegant, well-travelled woman with a strong work ethic. With each town she visited,

she collected recipes and techniques, all of which she shared with Malu. She educated her in gourmet Italian cuisine and helped her develop her already refined palate.

In the months preceding Damiano's birth, Malu and Alberto began to re-evaluate the objective of their centre. They were continuously spending money on the building and upkeep of their property, and survival by donations had become a withered ideal. With the impending arrival of a baby, Alberto needed to find more practical means of supporting his family. A friend working in a tourism office in Perugia introduced them to a new concept throughout Italy called Azienda Agrituristica, or Country House. Essentially,

farmers and landowners producing agricultural products were establishing themselves as small scale hotels. In addition, a number of grants from the Comunita Europea were available.

The appeal of this option was that, while they would be under a more formal umbrella, they would still have the freedom to preserve the distinctiveness they had sought since the beginning. Friends and family members teased them by saying they were selling their souls to capitalism and prosperity, but Malu and Alberto knew from the beginning that would not be the case. Their goal was to provide guests with an intimate, comfortable setting and fulfilling vegetarian cuisine, never to build a luxury resort and food factory, which they could have easily done given the natural beauty and substantial acreage of the property. As a Country House, they could continue to build creatively on their core purpose with the added security that the new title gave to them. It was a marriage of reality and idealism; of keeping their feet firmly planted while daring to dream and be original

and imaginative. Years later, many of the same friends who teased them saw Montali as a triumph and ventured to build their own Country Houses.

Piece by piece, Malu and Alberto continued to work and build on the Country House Montali over the following two decades. The small hotel, literally off the beaten track, steadily gained more attention and recognition across Western Europe and North America. Along with the healthy stream of newcomers, frequent guests returned year after year seeking an experience wholly emblematic of the rustic, undisturbed Italian countryside. Because Montali is a ceaseless labour of faith and love, the atmosphere exudes a peaceful, hopeful energy that settles into any individual who passes through.

For the first time in nearly 20 years, Malu and Alberto relaxed throughout the entire winter of 2004. There were no additional walls that needed to be erected, buildings to be constructed or pressing logistical issues to deal with. In the warmth of their stonewall home, they curled up with their son by the fireplace, now working, reading peacefully and pushing any thought of the following season to the furthest corners of their minds. Later, there would be considerable rebuilding or expansion projects and stressful bureaucratic issues to attend to. In the interim, though, the Musacchio family indulged in a well-deserved escape.

ARCHITECTURE

A few pages of this book are going to be dedicated to architecture. I imagine people will think "Why should a cookery book mention architecture as a food concept?" There is a reason why. Before becoming a chef, my wife was actually, in fact, an architect, and together we designed the restaurant, the hotel, the rooms and the professional kitchen as well.

In a way we had to apply her architectural expertise to the cooking profession, necessitating building a working restaurant kitchen.

But why a chapter about this? The reason is quite simple. People are cooking less and less. The quality of home cooking has never been so bad. People buy cookery books, and watch cookery programmes, while sitting on the sofa eating fish and chips.

Certainly, there are some historical and sociological reasons for this: the lack of time, the rush of modern life, and ...... architecture.

Have you ever noticed how a modern house is generally designed? With the cost increasing, houses have often turned into match boxes and the place that has been most sacrificed is THE KITCHEN. Kitchens literally turn into small wardrobes, with the sink reminding one of being on a train and about the size of a microwave. And where are they?

In the darkest corners of the whole house – a kind of cookery jail!! Who is going to work there? No one. So this is why there is this architecture section in this book. If we want to improve our cookery skills we should be able to do it and we should be able to do it in an acceptable way.

Kitchens should be in a well lit charming part of the house, not in the greenhouse or on the balcony!!

In ancient times, if you look at typical rural houses, the kitchen was the centre of the community life, with a big fireplace where everybody loved sitting on long winter nights, enjoying the cooking and later on eating with all the family. Now a 35" plasma television has taken the place of the fireplace, with the sofa in front of it, and this has pushed the cookery corner into the most hated, darkest corner of the house. No one wants to be there trapped, and families end up spending as little time as possible in those awful kitchens.

This surely means very poor quality food and, unfortunately, as little time together as possible.

The kitchen as a "momento" of unity expired, too.

This section should serve as a hint to all builders, architects and people in the process of renovating their houses to start designing buildings in a different way. There are some splendid

burners nowadays on the market that can beautifully furnish any house.

Kitchen furniture as well has become more and more elegant and sophisticated. You can now build some kitchens that look like modern art! You should never feel ashamed to invite friends to join you in your kitchen. You should always show it off with pride. And remember, a working kitchen is always the warmest place in the house – a place where you can have many lovely conversations.

What my wife, as an architect and chef, would suggest is NOT to separate the spaces of the kitchen from the living room.

Especially if your house is relatively small! This is a very good secret to make any house look bigger.

Do NOT isolate the kitchen and, please do NOT isolate the cook!!

Our own house is surely not large and our beautiful brick kitchen is definitely part of the living room. Our guests always enjoy pleasant conversations whilst my wife produces some of her fabulous recipes!

Mmmmmmm! All the great smells with the sound of sautéing.

Of course, then you will have to invite your guests for dinner, and rest assured you will always have a lot of friends!!!

A. M.

Running a vegetarian business has never been an easy task. Many restaurants close after a short time and this always saddens me. We have also gone through some difficult times but in our case the reasons were more bureaucratic than due to business problems. Here follows one of the most interesting gems of bureaucratic stupidity, which finally ended up being studied in law colleges in Brussels as a case of the 'system' against the single individual.

Our hotel, being a country hotel, is categorized as 'Agriturismo' in our region, and this means a farm with a hotel on its own land which consequently pays a little less tax as it is set in a rural area.

The law requires that we have to produce some of the agricultural products for the restaurant by ourselves to be classified so. With 1,500 olive trees and a big kitchen garden we have never had any problem accomplishing the requirements of the law. Still, some years ago, just after a famous earthquake that literally emptied the whole region of possible tourists (and with the understandable economic consequences), we went through one of the funniest bureaucratic nightmares in the history of law.

As I said, the regional law required us to grow some agricultural products on our 25-acre farm. But all of a sudden, the local agricultural department decided to tighten up this law as there were too many agriturismi popping up. The new law required not only some agricultural products to be produced in-situ but also a certain quantity of animals to be raised on the farm to provide the meat for the restaurant clients. In our case, considering the size of our restaurant, it was about 600 chickens or 200 sheep. This was what, out of the blue, the local authority expected of us.

You can imagine how pleased I was when I came to know about this new law. And, of course, not being willing to kill any of those 200 sheep, being a vegetarian myself, I started thinking of how many thousands they would become in a short time.

The idea of raising all those stinky chickens, which I could already imagine messing everywhere, destroying my gardens, making lots of noise and making my life hell, was quite terrifying to me. The major point, of course, was that I wasn't using any meat in my restaurant, and for the law to demand that I had animals for serving as meat sounded at least a little strange to me.

The idea of training them to dance the samba on the restaurant tables to entertain the clients proved to be too complicated, so we decided to fight this injustice. I wrote to 'La Repubblica', the major Italian newspaper, reporting the matter and, of course, the journalists loved this unusual story and published it with a comment underneath stating that it doesn't often happen that vegetarians are requested to raise animals for meat purposes in a vegetarian resort.

This was a wrong move.

The local office didn't like it at all. Within 20 days, we received an official communication in which they told us that our restaurant had been shut down since we were not complying with the new regulations of meat production!!!

You can imagine our reactions, and this was just after an event, like the earthquake, which literally put the tourism economy on its knees – including our small business. Nevertheless, as the son of an army general, I never take surrender as an answer. I was born to fight! I spent the next three days locked in my office writing to everyone I could think of all over the world. After another week, a second article of mine appeared in 'La Repubblica' and, if the previous one was playful, the second was a real 'j'accuse' of modern time. It has to be said that the funny story had intrigued many readers of the first issue. To see another 'episode' straight away, and with that kind of reprisal from the local authority, made the 'novella' a real success.

The answer didn't take too long, in fact. Two hundred faxes of protest (it was still fax times) arrived in the local office. Two senators took my side and called the local bureaucrats – making quite a big mess. The President of the Republic himself, also wrote to them (I jealously keep a copy of the letter) asking them to "Pay better attention to this case". And, the icing on the cake, was the Minister of Agriculture (we are under the Agricultural Department) asking for a Parliamentary Debate about this subject…Wow! The stupid little case of those vegetarian bastards made a fuss all the way up to the top political leader of the country. This was one thing that hadn't been taken into consideration by the local officer. Oops!

I got a call from the Mayor of our local town a few days later, saying, "Mr Musacchio, the law has been changed …. but please could you tell me how you managed to do that? It generally takes two years to have a law changed." Of course, after that, the reputation of some vegetarians being a real nuisance grew. Still, the politicians had to realise that it is better not to irritate the vegetarians too much.

They may not eat meat, but they can still bite!!

A. M.

Antipasti
STARTERS

BRUSCHETTA MISTA

Olive oil makers eat only unsalted bread with their oil during the late autumn and early winter after the olives are first pressed. The bread is first baked in a wood-burning stove, then sliced and toasted over a charcoal grill. While still hot, it is rubbed with a fresh garlic clove and served drizzled with the oil maker's finest extra virgin olive oil and a sprinkle of salt. This is the original and true bruschetta and the centuries-old method is still commonly found throughout Tuscany and Umbria. This simple, fine dish is often mispronounced. The correct pronunciation is 'brusketta'.

Serves 6   Ⓔ   *75 minutes*

MUSHROOM BRUSCHETTA

4 tablespoons extra virgin olive oil

1 sprig rosemary

2 garlic cloves, smashed

450 g (1 lb) mushrooms, chopped

1 tablespoon chopped parsley

Salt to taste

———

Heat the olive oil, rosemary and garlic in a sauté pan until the garlic begins to colour. Add the mushrooms and cook over a high heat for 5 minutes, or until the liquid has evaporated and the mushrooms are browned and crispy. Remove from the heat, remove the garlic and rosemary and cool completely. Add the chopped parsley and salt and set aside.

TOMATO BRUSCHETTA

300 g (11 oz) cherry tomatoes, rinsed and sliced

1 teaspoon oregano

1 garlic clove, gently smashed

4 tablespoons extra virgin olive oil

4 fresh basil leaves, chopped

Salt and pepper to taste

———

Toss all the ingredients together in a bowl 30 minutes before serving. Season to taste and set aside.

WALNUT GARLIC BRUSCHETTA

6 tablespoons walnuts, roughly chopped

1 garlic clove, minced

Salt and white pepper

5 tablespoons extra virgin olive oil

———

Combine all the ingredients. Set aside.

RADICCHIO BRUSCHETTA

140 g or 1 small radicchio, ribs removed and julienned

1 tablespoon chopped walnuts

4 tablespoons extra virgin olive oil

Salt, white pepper and black pepper

½ teaspoon balsamic vinegar

½ teaspoon lemon juice

——————

Combine all the ingredients in a bowl right before serving to retain the freshness of the leaves.

ROCKET PARMESAN BRUSCHETTA

100 g (3½ oz) rocket, roughly chopped

4 tablespoons coarsely grated Parmesan

Salt and white pepper

8 tablespoons extra virgin olive oil

——————

Combine all the ingredients in a bowl right before serving to retain the freshness of the leaves.

BRUSCHETTA

1 loaf Italian bread, sliced into 30 pieces of 8 mm (⅓") thickness

3 cloves garlic, peeled, for brushing

——————

Preheat the oven to Gas Mark 4/180°C/350°F. Spread the walnut garlic mixture over six slices of bread. Line the six slices along with the remaining slices of bread on a baking sheet and bake for 5 minutes. The bread should be crunchy on the outside and still soft and chewy in the middle. Remove from the oven and gently rub the garlic over the untopped toasted bread.

Lightly press one side of a piece of toasted bread in the oil of the tomato bruschetta mixture to soak. Top the same side with a portion of the tomatoes and repeat with five more slices. Follow the same pattern with the remaining bruschetta mixtures, using six slices of bread for each type.

Arrange the bruschetta on a large platter or individual plates and serve.

FICHI RIPIENI CARAMELLATI

Caramelised figs. An adventurous sweet and sour taste, made even more interesting by the crunchy caramel.

Serves 6 Ⓔ *15 minutes*

INGREDIENTS

100 g (3½ oz) Mascarpone
40 g (1½ oz) Gorgonzola
40 g (1½ oz) Tomino di Mucca or Brie
12 fresh figs
Butter, at room temperature
Brown sugar
24 roasted walnut halves
1 quantity Orange Sauce (see page 30)

———

Mix the cheeses with a fork or hand-held mixer until very creamy. Scoop into a piping bag.

Wash and dry each fig. With a small, sharp knife, make a shallow cross-like incision through the skin, starting from the top of the fig and stopping right before the bottom (do not cut through the whole fig). Rub butter over the surface of each fig and roll in brown sugar. Place the figs on a heat-proof surface (like the top of a casserole dish) and caramelise the outside with a blow torch. Wait until the figs are cool enough to handle, then cut three-quarters of the way through each one, following the incisions. Stuff each fig with a walnut half, fill with cheese from the piping bag and top with the remaining walnuts. Serve with warm Orange Sauce.

TARTINE DEGUSTAZIONE

A couple of great recipes if you need something cold to serve during cocktail hour or to welcome guests before an important meal. A nice combination of colours as well.

Serves 8 (M) *40 minutes & 30 minutes chilling & 1 hour for resting salad*

DOUGH

200 g (7 oz) Italian '00' flour, plus more for dusting
Pinch of salt

100 g (3½ oz) butter, softened
3 tablespoons water

———

Combine the flour and salt on a flat surface and make a well in the centre. Add the butter and water into the well and gently work with your fingertips until a dough begins to form. Incorporate by cutting through the dough with a pastry cutter and rolling back together, three or four times, until the texture and colour are even. Wrap in plastic film and refrigerate for 30 minutes.

POTATO SALAD

1 large potato
1 tablespoon Mayonnaise (see page 29)
1 tablespoon chopped green olives
1 tablespoon chopped red onions
1 tablespoon chopped gherkins

1 teaspoon chopped chives
1 teaspoon chopped parsley
2 teaspoons yoghurt
1 teaspoon extra virgin olive oil
Salt, white pepper and Tabasco to taste

———

Boil the potato to al dente and peel. Cool completely, then cut into 8 mm (⅓") cubes and place in a medium-sized bowl. Fold in the remaining ingredients gently (do not break up potato cubes) and season to taste. Cover the bowl with plastic film and rest for 1 hour before serving.

BEETROOT SALAD

1 beetroot, parboiled and cut into 8 mm (⅓") cubes
2 tablespoons yoghurt
½ teaspoon lemon juice

1 teaspoon chopped parsley
1 tablespoon creamy goat's cheese
Salt, black pepper and Tabasco to taste

———

Combine the ingredients in a medium-sized bowl and season to taste. Cover the bowl with plastic film and rest for 1 hour before serving.

ASSEMBLY

Butter 20 miniature pie tins. Between two layers of plastic film dusted with flour, roll out dough to a large disc 2 mm (⅛") in thickness. Remove the top layer of plastic. Place the pie tins upside-down over the dough and use a pie cutter or knife to cut around the tins, allowing for a 1 cm (½") rim all around. Gently press each disc into the tins and remove excess dough from the rims. Pierce the base of each tin once with a fork and place on a large baking tray. Bake at Gas Mark 4/175°F/350°C for 12 minutes. Cool to room temperature and remove pastry from the pie tins. Fill half with potato salad and the other half with beetroot salad and serve.

CARPACCIO di RAPA ROSSA

An elegant and impressive beetroot carpaccio, this appetizer can be prepared within minutes. The sweetness of the beetroot is complemented by strong cheeses and black pepper, while the sharpness of the rocket adds to the interesting blend of flavours and textures.

Serves 6 E *15 minutes*

INGREDIENTS

330 g (11½ oz) beetroot, parboiled
Lemon juice
48 g (1½ oz) walnuts, chopped
3 tablespoons fresh parsley, chopped
Salt and pepper to taste
Extra virgin olive oil
60 g (2 oz) creamy goat's cheese
60 g (2 oz) mid-aged goat's cheese
100 g (3½ oz) rocket

———

Wearing disposable gloves, slice the beetroot into thin discs using a mandolin. Decoratively place the discs on individual plates to form larger circles. Place one round in the centre of each. Drizzle with lemon juice and sprinkle the walnuts, parsley, salt, pepper and olive oil over the top.

Using a teaspoon, place small dollops of creamy goat's cheese on the beetroot. Sprinkle over grated mid-aged cheese. Add a small handful of rocket. Sprinkle with a little more salt and pepper, drizzle with a few drops of olive oil and serve.

RUSTICI alla RICOTTA

A delectable pie crust filled with a lemon and ricotta cheese fusion and topped with a light choux pastry.

Serves 8 (M) *60 minutes & 35 minutes baking*

BASE DOUGH

125 g (4½ oz) Italian '00' flour

1 flat tablespoon sugar

Zest of ½ lemon

55 g (2 oz) butter, melted and slightly cooled

3 tablespoons water

———

Sift the flour on to a flat work surface. Add the sugar and lemon zest and mix well. Create a small well in the centre and pour the butter and water inside. Using your fingertips only, slowly work the liquid into the dough until well incorporated. Gently gather the dough into a ball, wrap in plastic film and refrigerate for 15 minutes.

RICOTTA FILLING

175 g (6¼ oz) fresh ricotta

40 g (1½ oz) Scamorza, cut into 5 mm (¼") cubes

3 tablespoons grated Parmesan

1 egg yolk, lightly beaten

Zest of ½ lemon

Salt and black pepper to taste

———

Beat the ricotta with a fork until very creamy. Add the remaining ingredients, mix well and season to taste.

BIGNE DOUGH

42 g (1½ oz) butter, cubed

104 ml (3½ fl oz) water

56 g (2 oz) Manitoba flour

Pinch of salt

1½ eggs

———

Combine the butter and water in a saucepan over a medium heat. When the butter has melted and the liquid comes to a boil, remove from the heat and add the flour. Using a wooden spoon, mix the flour with the water and butter until combined. Place the saucepan back on the heat and continue stirring for 2 minutes or until the dough is shiny and begins to pull away from the sides and bottom. Remove from the heat and cool. Add the salt and then the eggs one at a time, mixing well after each addition. Cover and set aside.

ASSEMBLY

Butter eight miniature pie tins. Roll out the base dough between two sheets of plastic film that have been lightly floured until it is a wafer-thin disc. Place the pie tins upside down on the dough and use a small knife to cut around the tins, giving a 1 cm (½") border all around. Place the cut-out dough in the tins and press lightly around the bases and sides. Trim excess from the tins. Fill each with 1 tablespoon of the ricotta filling and flatten slightly. Spread the bigne batter over the ricotta to fill the tins. It should slightly resemble a dome, covering the rims. Bake at Gas Mark 4/180°C/350°F for 35 minutes. Remove, hold tin and gently release the pastry with the tip of a knife. Serve hot.

CAPPUCCINO di ASPARAGI

Whenever this dish is presented to unsuspecting guests, it is guaranteed to be a show stopper. Be sure to serve in champagne glasses and let your guests know it needs to be stirred. Great with a chilled prosecco wine.

Serves 4 (E) *30 minutes & 40 minutes simmering*

INGREDIENTS

1 bunch asparagus
30 g (1 oz) butter
Salt and pepper to taste
1 shallot, chopped finely
125 ml (4 fl oz) double cream
Nutmeg to taste

———

Break off the asparagus stems at the natural breaking point (each end will snap approximately 5 cm [2"] from the bottom when gently bent). Using a peeler, remove the fibrous parts of the stems. Leave the tip unpeeled. Reserve all the trimmings. In a pot of lightly salted boiling water, cook the asparagus for 3 minutes or until al dente. Transfer with a slotted spoon into an ice bath. Place the reserved trimmings in 500 ml (16 fl oz) of cooking water, cover and simmer for 40 minutes or until the stock has a full asparagus flavour. Set aside 300 ml (10 fl oz) of stock and keep warm.

Drain the cooled asparagus from the ice bath. Cut off the tips and set aside. Coarsely chop the stems. Sauté the tips with half the butter and season. In a separate pan, sauté the chopped stems with the shallots and remaining butter. Season and set aside.

TO SERVE

Reheat the tips and stems in separate sauté pans. Whip the cream with a hand-held mixer to soft peaks and transfer to a piping bag. Warm the stock if necessary. Place 1½ tablespoons of chopped asparagus stems in the bottom of a champagne flute. Fill with approximately 65 ml (2 fl oz) of warm stock. Add three asparagus tips into the glasses and top with a dollop of whipped cream and one more asparagus tip. Sprinkle with freshly ground nutmeg and serve immediately.

Aside from the cream, the stock and asparagus should be served warmed.

GASPACHO

A cool start to a summer meal, this classic Spanish treat is a chilled tomato soup laden with garden vegetables. Serve in martini glasses for an elegant presentation.

Serves 6 (E) *10 minutes & 1 hour chilling*

INGREDIENTS

1 slice of Italian bread, without crust

1 medium red bell pepper, deseeded

1 cucumber, peeled and soft inside scooped out

4 tomatoes, roughly chopped

½ garlic clove, sliced

3 teaspoons lemon juice

4 tablespoons extra virgin olive oil

2 teaspoons red wine vinegar

2 teaspoons balsamic vinegar

½ small onion, roughly chopped

Salt and black pepper to taste

A few drops of Tabasco

———

Cut the bread into cubes and blend until fine. Set aside.

Cube half the red pepper and half the cucumber for decoration. Roughly chop the remainder and mix with the remaining ingredients. Purée in a blender and pass through a wide sieve or colander to capture the seeds and skin of the vegetables. Mix in the breadcrumbs, taste for seasoning and refrigerate for at least 1 hour.

TO SERVE

Divide the liquid between six Martini glasses. Top with an ice cube and the red pepper and cucumber pieces, drizzle with olive oil and serve.

CRESPELLE FANTASIA

Light pancakes stuffed with an aubergine cream and served with a velvety cheese sauce. This wonderful dish is excellent in the winter, and the strong flavour and richness of the 'fonduta' goes well with a glass of vintage wine.

Serves 6 (M) *95 minutes*

CRÊPES

1 tablespoon butter, plus more for pan

150 ml (5 fl oz) milk

75 g (2¾ oz) flour

1 egg

Salt and black pepper to taste

24 parsley leaves

6 long chives

Melt the butter and cool to room temperature. Whisk in the milk, flour, egg, salt and pepper. Heat a non-stick 20 cm (8") skillet or crêpe pan over a medium heat. Spread 1 teaspoon of butter around the pan with a paper towel. Remove the pan from the heat and ladle 60 ml (2 fl oz) of batter into the pan, swirling to spread. Arrange four parsley leaves around the centre when the batter is still moist and place the pan back on the heat. Cook until one side is golden, flip and cook the other side in the same manner. Repeat with the remaining batter (makes six crêpes).

FILLING

1 shallot, chopped

1 garlic clove, chopped

1 sprig thyme, fresh

2 tablespoons extra virgin olive oil

2 aubergines, peeled and cubed

Salt and black pepper to taste

1 flat tablespoon chopped parsley

1 tablespoon creamy goat's cheese

Gently sauté the shallot, garlic and thyme in olive oil over a medium-low heat for 1 minute until soft. Add the aubergines, season with salt and pepper and cook. Stir occasionally until the aubergine is dry and very soft (approximately 25 minutes). Remove from the heat, add the parsley and cool to room temperature before mixing in the goat's cheese.

FONDUTA

100 g (3½ oz) Fontina cheese, cut into small cubes

100 ml (3½ fl oz) milk

1 egg yolk

1 tablespoon butter

2 teaspoons cornflour

One hour before serving, combine the Fontina and milk in a saucepan away from the heat. Mix in the egg yolk, butter and cornflour. Cook in a double boiler over simmering water, stirring continuously, for about 20 minutes. Work the cheese with the back of a spoon to melt completely.

ASSEMBLY

Dip the chives in a pot of simmering water for 1 second and transfer to an ice bath. Cool completely. Lay out the crêpes on a flat surface and spoon the filling into the centre of each. Bundle each one like a small bag and tie by wrapping a chive around twice and tying the ends. Transfer to a baking tray lined with parchment paper, cover with another sheet of parchment and heat at Gas Mark 4/180°C/350°F for 10 minutes. Serve hot alongside the Fonduta.

CRUDITE di PERE e MELONE

A pear and melon salad served with a balsamic vinaigrette glaze and honey, topped with Fossa and Castelmagno cheeses. The unique combination of savoury, sweet and acidic tastes is as easy as it is unexpectedly delicious.

Serves 6   Ⓔ   *15 minutes*

INGREDIENTS

6 small pears, peeled and thinly sliced

1 small cantaloupe melon, peeled and thinly sliced

Lemon juice

Extra virgin olive oil

Honey

Salt

Balsamic Reduction Sauce (see page 26)

6 slices each of Fossa and Castelmagno, or aged sheep's cheese

Chives

Black pepper to taste

———

Decoratively place slices of pear and melon on six serving plates. Drizzle lemon juice, olive oil, honey, salt and Balsamic Sauce over the fruit. Top with one slice of each cheese and garnish with a single chive. Sprinkle with pepper and serve immediately.

GUACAMOLE alla MONTALI

The Montali variation remains true to the well-known Mexican dish, adding a touch of Italian flair to set it apart.

Serves 6 **E** *20 minutes*

GUACAMOLE

1 ripe avocado

1 tomato, peeled and chopped with seeds removed

1 tablespoon extra virgin olive oil

Juice of ½ lemon

½ teaspoon Dijon mustard

Salt and pepper to taste

_____

Halve the avocado lengthwise with a small knife, moving around the stone. Using your hands, rotate the halves in opposite directions to split. Scoop out the avocado flesh with a spoon, reserving the stone. Mash the avocado well with a fork. Combine with the remaining ingredients and mix thoroughly. Place the reserved stone in the bowl with the guacamole, cover with plastic film and refrigerate.

CORN AND BEAN SALAD

150 g (5 oz) sweet corn, cooked

250 g (8 oz) cannellini beans, cooked

2 tablespoons red bell pepper, deseeded and chopped

1 small shallot, chopped

2 teaspoons lemon juice

4 tablespoons extra virgin olive oil

1 teaspoon balsamic vinegar

1 garlic clove, puréed

Salt, black pepper and white pepper to taste

A few drops of Tabasco

_____

Toss all the ingredients together in a bowl.

TO SERVE

1 tablespoon fresh parsley, chopped

1 tablespoon chives, chopped

_____

Discard the stone from the guacamole. Serve the corn and bean salad in individual glasses, topped with a dollop of guacamole and garnished with chopped parsley and chives.

TORRI di ZUCCHINE RIPIENE con CREMA di PISELLI

Courgette towers stuffed with a pea cream and roasted almonds. A sophisticated and eye-pleasing dish, where a nearly raw courgette shelters the soft purée, which contrasts with the crunchy almond texture.

Serves 6 (18 pieces)　Ⓔ　*25 minutes*

INGREDIENTS

3 courgettes
120 g (4 ½ oz) fresh peas
1 tablespoon extra virgin olive oil
Salt, black pepper and white pepper to taste
½ onion, sliced
1 tablespoon Mascarpone cheese
½ teaspoon lemon juice
1 tablespoon creamy goat's cheese
Almond slivers
Icing sugar

———

Level the ends of the courgettes and cut across into 5 cm (2") pieces. Halve each piece on a slight bias (see picture). Using an apple corer, remove the inside to create a tube-like effect. Cook the courgettes in a large pot of boiling water for 2 minutes then transfer to an ice bath to cool quickly. Drain over a colander and dry. Grill the courgette pieces, bias-side down, until grill marks are visible. Turn each piece 90° and continue to grill, creating a cross-hatched effect. Remove from the heat and set aside.

In a small pot, cook the peas with 1 tablespoon of olive oil, salt, white pepper, the onion and just enough water to cover until tender. Drain, remove the onion and discard, and purée the peas. Pass the purée through a sieve or food mill. Add the Mascarpone, lemon juice and goat cheese to the peas and mix well.

Toast the almond slivers in a pan over a low heat. When golden, lightly sprinkle over a small amount of icing sugar, just to sweeten, and toast for a few more seconds. Remove from the heat.

TO SERVE

Fill a piping bag with the pea purée. Arrange three courgette towers, bias-side up, on each of six serving plates and fill the insides with the purée. Top each courgette with almonds, black pepper, and a spot of olive oil and serve.

CRUDITE di SPINACI e RUCOLA

Spinach and rocket salad dressed with a hot garlic and caper sauce, served with dried tomatoes, black olives and a shaving of Parmesan cheese. This seamless combination of classic Mediterranean favourites makes for a surprisingly unique salad.

Serves 6   E   *15 minutes*

DRESSING

185 ml (6 fl oz) olive oil

30 capers (rinse well if packed in brine or vinegar)

6 garlic cloves, peeled and thinly sliced

———

Heat all ingredients over a low heat. In 8 minutes, or when the garlic begins to lightly caramelize, remove from the heat. The hot oil will continue to cook the garlic and capers.

SALAD

250 g (9 oz) spinach leaves, cleaned and dried

170 g (6 oz) rocket, cleaned and dried

Salt to taste

Olive oil to taste

Red wine vinegar to taste

24 seedless black olives

6 oil-packed sun-dried tomatoes, julienned

Parmigiano Reggiano shavings

Black pepper to taste

———

Toss the spinach and rocket with a sprinkling of salt, olive oil and red wine vinegar.

Divide the dressed greens between six serving plates. Spoon the garlic chips and capers over the greens, garnish evenly with the olives and sun-dried tomatoes, top with shavings of Parmigiano Reggiano and sprinkle with freshly ground black pepper. Serve immediately.

STUZZICHINI al FORMAGGIO e MELE VERDI

A delicate pastry teaser, a chunky mixture of creamy cheeses and Granny Smith apples are sandwiched between thin, bite-sized cheesy biscuits.

Serves 6 (12 pieces) (M) *25 minutes & 2 hours chilling*

DOUGH

100 g (3½ oz) Italian '00' flour

2 pinches salt

1 tablespoon grated Parmesan

50 g (1¾ oz) ricotta

4 tablespoons butter, at room temperature

1 egg yolk, for brushing

12 walnut halves

———

Combine the flour, salt and Parmesan on a flat surface and make a well in the centre. Add the ricotta and butter and work between your fingertips until the dough comes together. Roll into a ball and knead a few times. Wrap in plastic film and refrigerate for 2 hours. Roll out into a rectangle 3 mm (⅛") in thickness, large enough to cut 24 squares 6 cm (2½") in size. Place the squares 1 cm (½") apart on a baking sheet lined with parchment paper. Brush all 24 pastries with egg and top 12 with a walnut half. Bake at Gas Mark 4/180°C/350°F for 12 minutes or until golden-brown. Remove from the heat.

FILLING

28 g (1 oz) creamy goat's cheese

56 g (2 oz) Crescenza or Mascarpone

56 g (2 oz) ricotta

Salt and black pepper to taste

1 teaspoon extra virgin olive oil

1 teaspoon chopped chives

1 pinch paprika

¼ Granny Smith apple, cut into 5 mm (¼") cubes

———

Combine all the ingredients, except the apple, together and mix well until creamy. Transfer this cream into a piping bag with a medium tip and set aside.

TO SERVE

Pipe out the cream filling over the 12 walnut-free halves and layer the apple cubes over the cream. Top with the walnut-covered halves. Serve warm, two per person, with a crunchy mixed salad.

FRITTO MISTO

A variety of vegetables dipped in tempura batter and deep fried to crispness, this dish is typical of the Piedmont region.

Serves 6   Ⓜ   *50 minutes*

INGREDIENTS

1 or 2 Japanese aubergines, sliced horizontally into 12 x 5 mm (¼") slices

1 courgette, thinly sliced

2 medium onions, sliced thinly in rings

3 carrots, halved then julienned into 5 mm (¼") strips

3 peaches, thinly sliced

Vegetable oil for deep frying

Salt

Herb Yoghurt Sauce (see page 29)

SEMOLINO DOLCE

250 ml (8 fl oz) milk

1 tablespoon butter

2 tablespoons sugar

Grated zest of ½ lemon

Rind of ½ lemon

52 g (2 oz) semolina flour

Combine the milk, butter, sugar, lemon zest and rind in a saucepan and bring to a boil. Add the semolina flour and cook for 15 minutes, stirring continuously. Discard the rind and pour the mixture into a medium-sized loaf pan lined with damp parchment paper (the semolina should come 2.5 cm [1"] up the sides). Cover with more parchment paper and press well. Cool completely. When at room temperature, invert onto a flat surface and cut into 2.5 x 2.5 mm (1 x 1") squares, 5 mm (¼") thick.

IMPANATURA (BREADING)

6 tablespoons Italian '00' flour

3 eggs, lightly beaten with a pinch of salt

12 tablespoons breadcrumbs

Separate the three ingredients into separate wide bowls.

TEMPURA BATTER

10 tablespoons Italian '00' flour

4 tablespoons cornflour

220 ml (7 fl oz) beer

Pinch of salt

Mix all the ingredients together until smooth. Place in the freezer for a few minutes before using.

TO SERVE

Coat the aubergine and semolino dolce pieces first in flour, then egg, then breadcrumbs and line on a tray. The remaining vegetables and peach slices should be dipped into the tempura batter as they are fried. Heat the vegetable oil in two separate pots. In one pot, deep fry the aubergine first, then the semolina dolce. Deep fry the tempura-coated ingredients in the other pot, cooking the onions last. The julienned carrots can be fried in clumps. As they are cooked, transfer the fried foods to a tray lined with paper towels to drain and, except for the peaches and semolino dolce, season everything with salt. Serve with a dollop of Herb Yoghurt Sauce.

INSALATA del BOSCO

A fresh mushroom salad prepared with rocket, walnuts and Parmesan cheese. The rawness of this dish brings out the unique woody aroma and flavour of porcini mushrooms.

Serves 6 Ⓔ *10 minutes*

INGREDIENTS

6 small porcini mushrooms (others will also do)

24 walnut halves

6 handfuls of rocket

Juice of ½ lemon

6 tablespoons extra virgin olive oil

12 generous shavings of Parmigiano Reggiano

Black pepper, to taste

Thinly slice the Parmigiano Reggiano over a mandolin for best results.

Wipe the mushrooms with a damp towel to clean. Slice thinly using a mandolin, maintaining the mushroom outline. Split each walnut half down the centre.

Toss all the ingredients, except the Parmigiano Reggiano and pepper, in a bowl and transfer to a large serving dish.

Gently fluff up the salad with a fork, top with the Parmigiano Reggiano shavings and a sprinkle of pepper and serve.

CALZONI

This Neapolitan stuffed fried pastry literally translates as 'trousers'. Best when made with buffalo mozzarella.

Serves 8 Ⓜ *40 minutes & 70 minutes for resting dough*

DOUGH

375 g (13½ oz) Italian '00' flour, plus more for dusting
1 teaspoon salt
218 ml (7½ fl oz) warm water

1 tablespoon extra virgin olive oil
19 g (¾ oz) fresh yeast
1 pinch sugar

———

Combine the flour and salt in a large bowl. Create a well in the centre and add the water and olive oil. Add the yeast and sugar into the well and mix well using your fingertips. Work around the well to incorporate the flour until the dough comes together. Knead well until soft and elastic. Gently spread a few drops of oil around the surface of the dough, cover with a cloth and rest for 35 minutes in a warm, dry place. After the dough has rested, sprinkle the surface of the dough with flour and 'turn' it by pulling small portions of the dough around the edge towards the opposite side of the bowl. Once one full turn has been made, cover again and rest for 35 more minutes.

FILLING

180 g (6 oz) cherry tomatoes
½ teaspoon dry oregano
24 basil leaves, 12 chopped and 12 left whole
1 garlic clove, smashed and chopped

Salt and black pepper to taste
Extra virgin olive oil
110 g (4 oz) fresh mozzarella, drained

———

While the dough is resting, deseed and roughly chop the tomatoes. Set over a colander for 30 minutes to drain. Combine with the oregano, chopped basil, garlic, salt, pepper and two drops of extra virgin olive oil in a bowl. Cut the mozzarella into cubes about the same size as the chopped tomatoes, dry slightly and add to the filling mix.

ASSEMBLY

On a clean work surface dusted with flour, roll the dough out into a disc shape 3 mm (⅛") in thickness. With the use of a 8 cm (3") round cutter or a glass cup, cut out 24 rounds from the soft dough. Take each disc and place a full teaspoon of filling in the centre. Place half a whole basil leaf over the filling. Fold over half of the disc and seal using the teeth of a fork, gently pressing down so that it firmly seals the dough but does not break it. Place the calzoni on a tray lined with parchment paper and dusted with Grano Duro flour.

In a large pot, heat enough vegetable oil to cover the calzoni. When the oil is ready, gently place the calzoni in the pot. Allow one side to brown for about 1 minute before flipping over to cook the other side. When the calzoni are golden brown in colour, remove with a slotted spoon and drain on a tray lined with paper towels. Season with salt and serve immediately.

BIGNE con CREMA di FUNGHI

An Italian choux pastry stuffed with a mushroom cream sauce. This wonderful appetiser is complemented by a red port wine.

Serves 8 Ⓜ *40 minutes*

FILLING

448 g (16 oz) mushrooms

2 garlic cloves, 1 minced, the other whole

3 tablespoons extra virgin olive oil

Salt and pepper to taste

2 tablespoons Robiola cheese

1 tablespoon chopped parsley

———

Wipe the mushrooms with a damp cloth, trim the base of the stems and chop. Sauté all the garlic in 2 tablespoons of olive oil until it begins to brown, add the chopped mushrooms and cook over a high heat until any liquid has evaporated and the mushrooms are golden brown. Remove from the heat. Remove 2 tablespoons of cooked mushrooms for garnishing. Discard the whole garlic and purée the mushrooms in a blender. Season to taste with salt and pepper. Fold in the remaining ingredients and set aside.

CHOUX PASTRY

53 ml (2¾ fl oz) water

28 g (1 oz) butter, cut into cubes

Pinch of salt

28 g (1 oz) Manitoba flour

1 small egg

———

Heat the water, butter and salt in a pot over a medium heat, melting the butter completely. As soon as the liquid comes to a boil, remove from the heat. Add the flour all at once and whisk well until combined. Return to the heat and continue to whisk for an additional 30 seconds, or until the dough pulls away from the sides and bottom of the pot. Remove from the heat and cool slightly. Mix in the egg with a wooden spoon, incorporating completely.

Transfer into a piping bag with a 7 mm (3") tip and pipe out ½ tablespoon amounts onto a silicon mat or baking sheet. Lightly brush the top of each pastry with water and bake at Gas Mark 4/190°C/350°F for 10 minutes. Cool completely.

ASSEMBLY

Using a serrated knife, carefully slice off the top quarter of each pastry and set aside. Use a piping bag to fill each base with mushroom purée. Replace the top quarter over each bigne, dot the surface with more mushroom purée, and gently press the reserved mushroom slices on to the top. Place on a baking tray, cover and heat at Gas Mark 4/175°C/350°F for 7 minutes. Serve hot.

CRUDITE di ZUCCHINE e SALSA allo YOGURT e ERBE

A great summer dish to refresh you or give you a lift. Light and low fat.

Serves 6   E   *10 minutes*

INGREDIENTS

6 small courgettes

Salt and white pepper to taste

Juice of ½ lemon

4 tablespoons extra virgin olive oil

1 quantity Herb Yoghurt Sauce

3 tablespoons almond slivers, toasted

―――

Trim the ends of the courgettes and slice thinly on a mandolin. Keep refrigerated. When ready to serve, overlap the courgette slices around a plate. Season with salt and white pepper and drizzle over the lemon juice and olive oil. Let it all marinate for 5 minutes.

HERB YOGHURT SAUCE

1 quantity

150 ml (5 fl oz) double cream lightly whipped

150 ml (5 fl oz) yoghurt

1 small garlic clove

1 tablespoon mixed herbs (chives, thyme, rosemary and basil), finely chopped

3 tablespoons extra virgin olive oil

Salt and black pepper

2 teaspoons lemon juice

―――

Partly foam the double cream and mix in the remaining ingredients. Refrigerate until needed.

TO SERVE

Pour the Herb Yoghurt Sauce over the salad, sprinkle with almonds and serve.

PANZANELLA

A lovely summer dish with an ancient rural tradition, Panzanella originates from the old Italian habit of not letting anything go to waste. It is still a great and healthy Mediterranean way to get rid of old bread by combining it with seasonal ingredients. Definitely a dish to be enjoyed in the summer.

Serves 6 Ⓜ *25 minutes*

INGREDIENTS

4 slices bread, cut into 1 cm (½") cubes

10 tablespoons extra virgin olive oil

Salt and pepper to taste

6 cherry tomatoes cut into quarters

1 cucumber, peeled and cut into 5 mm (¼") cubes

1 carrot, cut into 5 mm (¼") cubes

1 courgette, cut into 5 mm (¼") cubes

1 celery stalk, fibrous parts removed and sliced over a mandolin

1 small head of Romaine lettuce, roughly chopped

1 small radicchio, roughly chopped

200 g (7 oz) Pecorino di Pienza, cut into 5 mm (¼") cubes

1 garlic clove, puréed

1 small onion, chopped

1 flat tablespoon oregano

10 basil leaves, roughly chopped

1 tablespoon red wine vinegar

Juice of ½ lemon

150 g (5½ oz) buffalo mozzarella

———

Toss the bread with 2 tablespoons of olive oil and season with salt and pepper. Briefly toast at Gas Mark 4/180°C/350°F for 1 minute until crunchy, but not tough. Transfer to a large bowl and cool completely before adding the remaining olive oil and all other ingredients, except for the mozzarella. Transfer to a large serving dish, top with the mozzarella, sprinkle with more pepper and serve.

ASPARAGI con SALSA all' ARANCIA

Asparagus served with an orange sauce. A velvety acid flavour to contrast with the dominating asparagus taste.

Serves 6 Ⓔ *30 minutes*

INGREDIENTS

1 bunch asparagus

2 tablespoons walnuts, chopped

2 radicchio leaves, julienned

Extra virgin olive oil

Black pepper to taste

————

Break off the asparagus stems at their natural breaking point (the end will snap approximately 5 cm [2"] from the bottom when gently bent). Using a peeler, remove the fibrous parts of the stems, leaving the tips unpeeled. Bring a pot of lightly salted water to a boil. Cook the asparagus for 2 minutes or until al dente. Transfer to an ice bath using a slotted spoon. When cool, remove from the water and dry over paper towels.

ORANGE SAUCE

2 navel oranges

1 tablespoon cornflour

3 tablespoons white wine

1 teaspoon lemon juice

21 g (¾ oz) butter, at room temperature

Salt and white pepper to taste

————

Squeeze the oranges to get approximately 250 ml (8 fl oz) of juice. In a small saucepan, combine the orange juice, cornflour, white wine and lemon juice and cook over a medium heat until thickened, approximately 3 minutes. Remove from the heat and add the butter in teaspoon increments, continuously stirring until sauce is smooth and creamy. Season to taste and keep warm.

TO SERVE

Lay the asparagus on individual plates, placing four stems in a row. Pour warm Orange Sauce across the centre of the asparagus and sprinkle with the chopped walnuts. Garnish with a bed of radicchio at the base of the stems, a drizzle of olive oil and freshly ground black pepper. Serve immediately.

POLENTA TARAGNA

A variation of the typical corn recipe from the northeast of Italy. Polenta Taragna, a blend of common corn flour and buckwheat, is layered with mushrooms and a broad bean purée with a drizzle of balsamic vinaigrette on the side.

Serves 6   Ⓜ   *60 minutes*

POLENTA

240 ml (8 fl oz) milk
240 ml (8 fl oz) water
2 tablespoons butter
100 g (3½ oz) Polenta Taragna*

30 g (1 oz) grated Parmesan
20 g (¾ oz) grated Pecorino di Pienza
Pinch of salt

———

Heat the milk, water and butter in a saucepan to a boil. Immediately add the polenta flour and cook for 40 minutes, stirring frequently. Add the cheeses and salt and continue cooking until the cheese has melted. Line a 23 x 10 cm (9 x 4") loaf pan with damp parchment paper covering all sides. Pour the polenta into the prepared pan and tap the bottom against the table to flatten and get rid of any air bubbles. Cover with parchment paper and press down with your hands to even. Cool to room temperature.

MUSHROOM SLICES

2 garlic cloves
3 tablespoons extra virgin olive oil
300 g (10½ oz) mushrooms, sliced

Salt and black pepper to taste
1 teaspoon chopped parsley

———

Sauté the garlic in the olive oil over a high heat. When the garlic begins to colour, add the mushrooms and cook until golden. Season with salt and pepper and add the parsley last. Set aside.

BROAD BEAN PURÉE

35 g (1½ oz) dried broad beans, rinsed
½ carrot, halved lengthwise
2 garlic cloves
½ medium onion, peeled and quartered
1 sprig parsley

2 tablespoons extra virgin olive oil
Salt to taste
250 ml (9 fl oz) water
1 tablespoon lemon juice
1 tablespoon tahini

———

Combine the beans, carrot, 1 whole garlic clove, onion, parsley, 1 tablespoon olive oil, salt and water in a large pot and cook over a low heat for 40 minutes, or until the beans are tender. Remove the vegetables, garlic, parsley and excess liquid. Purée the beans in a blender. Purée remaining garlic clove and add to beans along with the lemon juice, tahini and remaining olive oil. Season to taste. Cover and set aside.

ASSEMBLY

100 g (3½ oz) Ghee (see page 28)
Balsamic Reduction Sauce (see page 26)

Truffle Sauce** (see page 36)

———

Invert the polenta on to a cutting board and cut into 5 mm (¼") slices. Brown both sides of each slice in clarified butter (ghee) until golden and cool on a tray lined with parchment paper. Spread ½ tablespoon of Broad Bean Purée over one polenta slice and top with mushroom slices. Cover the mushrooms with another slice of polenta and repeat layering. Cover with a third and final slice of polenta. Repeat with the remaining slices and place on a baking sheet lined with parchment paper.

To serve, cover the Polenta Taragna with aluminium foil and reheat at Gas Mark 4/180°C/350°F for 5 minutes. Top with ½ teaspoon of Truffle Sauce and serve with Balsamic Reduction Sauce on the side.

*If Polenta Taragna is unavailable, substitute with plain polenta.
**If Truffle Sauce is not available, substitute with Caper Parsley Sauce (see Basics).

DAMIANO

Following strict instructions, 11-year-old Damiano arranged generous slices of cheese with bread around a plate and brought it out to his father on the veranda. "Thank you, Dami," Alberto said. He looked at his staff and continued, "I love my son! Always so charming and polite!" He looked down at his plate, frowned, and thundered, "Damiano! Don't ever bring out a plate without a fork! Learn to do things properly!"

Personal archive picture

Animatedly, his son bounded into the kitchen and returned with fork in hand in seconds. Alberto affectionately patted his son's cheek before turning his attention to his lunch.

Damiano, extraordinarily mature for his age, is an exact blend of both parents. Like his mother, he bounds about with verve and takes pleasure in the smallest acts of everyday life. From his father, he inherited the determination and focus to start and finish any project he tackles. He is quick to invent fantastic and hilarious stories with comic timing, eager to help in the kitchen or in the grounds and generous with his toys and belongings. He is the joy of the Country House Montali and the marvel of those who meet him. But mostly, he is still an 11-year-old boy with 11-year-old interests, sensitive and protective to the needs of his parents and resentful when his time with them is cut short. He is a young man defined by his own character and the nature in which he has been raised.

Damiano was born on February 22, 1994, after a complicated pregnancy. He was a healthy baby boy who looked exactly like Alberto. Despite warnings given by numerous doctors and specialists, Malu was determined to raise her son on a vegetarian diet. After the first few months of milk, she would incorporate vegetables into Damiano's diet, respecting his choice to accept or reject different ones. Damiano happily devoured the lentils and, later, after tasting pasta with light tomato sauce, rejected soft foods altogether for solids at the age of nine months. Doctors were amazed at the baby's growth and his alert responsiveness to stimulation. Eleven years later, he already towers over most of his classmates and continues to grow.

One November, the Musacchio family was taking their annual month-long post-season holiday, this year in Brazil. Damiano was five years old at the time and already quite perceptive. At dinner one evening, he was sitting between his parents at a table full of adults. Malu's sister-in-law, a wine aficionado, ordered a bottle of red wine. The waiter brought it to their table and poured a small amount in her glass to taste. She flamboyantly swirled her glass, sniffed deeply before sipping, swished the wine in her mouth and nodded in approval. A few minutes later, the same waiter began pouring Damiano's coca-cola into his glass. When it was partially full, Damiano took his glass, swirled it, sniffed deeply before tasting and nodded to the waiter in approval, sending the table into howls of laughter.

Damiano's personality is based on both his innate character as well as carefully observing everything he has seen. His parents decided early on that the best education they could provide their son was to open his eyes to the whole world from a very young age. Easily one of the most well travelled children, he has been to Australia, Brazil, Lisbon, London and

five Southeast Asian countries. Staying in anywhere from a simple village inn to a five star hotel in a major metropolitan city, he studies the rich culture and history of each town with his mother. By necessity, he assimilates easily with locals and effortlessly makes friends wherever he goes. When he is alone, he entertains himself by inventing science-fiction tales of fantastic universes. His mind is coloured by the rich civilizations and experiences he has seen at first hand; his imagination is alive and vibrant.

At his age, he has an incredible work ethic. Along with witnessing the hours his parents put into the family-run business, he takes note of how various staff members work. This chef always works neatly, while the other never picks up his own mess. That girl is always happy while the other one is always depressed. He listens to his parents as they discuss what they admire and value and he takes their work philosophy as his own.

Unfortunately, living and breathing the hospitality lifestyle wears Damiano down as well. Late one Sunday evening during dinner service, Damiano was sitting on a bench outside with his feet up and arms wrapped around his legs. He was staring sadly into space, uncharacteristically unresponsive to other people. Malu walked outside and put her arm around him and encouraged him to talk to her. He looked up at her and said simply, "Mamma, sometimes I really hate this." It was Sunday, the day his mother took off to spend with her son. Out of necessity she was downstairs working in the kitchen. His one day with her was lost.

Pressing matters and small emergencies continually interrupt the precious time that he has to spend with his parents. But rather than shut himself off, Damiano remains eager to open up and build personal relationships with nearly anyone who comes to work at Montali.

Being raised around food inevitably heightens one's awareness and understanding of it.

Damiano's passions might be motorbike racing and soccer, but food is a predestined part of his life. Though he is most fond of simple foods like slabs of Parmigiano Reggiano or pasta e ceci, he can also eat plate upon plate of spicy Oriental-style noodles or curry-flavoured couscous.

He appreciates new and uncommon flavours, but doesn't always enjoy overcomplicated smorgasbords of dishes. His ability to distinguish textures and flavours, to discriminate between different components in a dish, is beyond most adults. When Damiano has tomato sauce, he discerns the quality of the tomato, not always the overall flavour.

Malu and Alberto explained early on the very simple reasons why they were vegetarians. Not only was it an issue of health, but they also did not like the idea of another living creature losing its life so that others could eat. However, they stressed, that did not mean that they were any better or worse than others. Growing up as a vegetarian in a small town in Italy, Damiano has faced occasional bantering from classmates who do not understand this 'odd' eating behaviour.

"Eww! What is that?" one of them exclaimed one afternoon, calling everyone's attention to Damiano's lunch. Malu had made him a sandwich with several slices of Seitan, his favourite. "Excuse me," Damiano quickly retorted. "Have you ever tasted this? Do you even know what it is?" The classmate shook his head sheepishly. Damiano exchanged a knowing glance with Paolo, his best friend and son of the local butcher, before returning to his lunch. While Damiano's classmates may not wholly understand his eating habits, none can deny the quality of Malu's cooking. For his February birthday, Malu always prepares a spectacular feast that all the schoolchildren look forward to for months in advance.

Should Damiano choose to stay a vegetarian for the rest of his life is a choice that Malu and

Alberto have left completely to him. There may come a time when he grows curious about tasting new things, and he may want to change that aspect of his lifestyle entirely. The same is true for his career. If he wanted to take over the Country House Montali as an adult, his parents would be thrilled, but it would never be something they pushed on him. Damiano has always been encouraged to be his own person and seek his own path, and his parents have always done their best to guide him in the right direction while respecting his decisions, likes and dislikes. They help him to distinguish between what he needs and what he wants, to work hard towards various goals and to always use his mind as the greatest tool in life.

Malu and Alberto continue to teach him about food and hospitality at a steady pace. Already, he can make his own fresh pasta, ciabatta and pizzas, open wine bottles and serve with dignity. He became a 'star' one day in Earls Court when the old chef Gennaro Contaldo called him up on stage. Since Damiano had nothing to do while his parents and staff were briefing before their cookery course for each day, he began to kindly and politely offer his help to this famous Italian chef. He was doing it for fun, but ended up becoming a real help to Gennaro, who was happy to have an extra, and excellent, helper in such busy times. On the last day of the event, at the moment when Gennaro was handing over to Alberto for the cookery classes, he called Damiano to the stage with him, in front of a big crowd of people. He signed his cookery book with best wishes and said to the big British crowd aware of the special moment: "The reason why we have so many good chefs in Italy is that we start to train them young. Please, applause for the youngest chef of Italy and Britain!" A few eyes turned wet seeing something very similar to the 'handing over of offices'.

One cool August evening before dinner, Alberto was sitting on the veranda with a few guests and called out to his son. "Damiano! Three espressos!" Damiano set the tray with demi-glace spoons, serving sugar and base plates before starting the espresso so that everything would be ready. He carried out the porcelain-laden tray and gently placed it on the table before his father. The service was perfect, and Alberto shared a proud, quiet smile with his son as the guests raved.

Damiano, seeing that a beautiful 12-year-old would be having dinner at the restaurant that night, left his father and raced upstairs to get ready. Fifteen minutes later, freshened with a shower, light cologne and hair gel, he put on his best shirt and jeans and emerged downstairs to help his mother with dinner. The kitchen staff grinned and Malu sighed wistfully. "Amore di mamma. Now it begins. Oh, my son is growing up so fast!"

Primi
FIRST COURSES

BIPARMENTIER

A velvety combination of two classic soups. At the end of the last century, a disease destroyed potato crops all over Europe resulting in thousands of casualties. A French scientist, Monsieur Parmentier, discovered that potato plants near copper mines had not been affected. Parmentier found that treating potato crops with copper sulphate protected them from the disease. This delicious potato and leek soup is named after that scientist. Here it is served with a pumpkin soup. Great with a mild red wine.

Serves 6   Ⓔ   *45 minutes*

PARMENTIER (POTATO AND LEEK SOUP)

1 leek, white and light green parts only

1 tablespoon extra virgin olive oil

1 tablespoon butter

300 g (10½ oz) potatoes, peeled and thinly sliced

30 g (1 oz) green olives, coarsely chopped

1 tablespoon parsley, coarsely chopped

780 ml (26 fl oz) Vegetable Stock (see page 36)

1 tablespoon single cream

Salt and black pepper to taste

———

Clean the leek well and coarsely chop. Cook in the oil and butter in a large pot over a medium heat for 2 minutes. When soft, but not coloured, add the potatoes, olives, parsley and stock and simmer until the potatoes are tender and thoroughly cooked.

Remove from the heat. Purée in batches in a blender until the soup is completely smooth. Pour through a sieve to catch any remaining chunks, then pour back into a clean pot. Stir in the single cream and season with salt and black pepper. Cover and set aside until ready to serve.

ZUCCA (PUMPKIN SOUP)

1 leek, white and light green parts only

1 small shallot, finely chopped

1 tablespoon extra virgin olive oil

1 tablespoon butter

250 g (9 oz) pumpkin, peeled and cut into 1 cm (½") cubes

1 potato, peeled and thinly sliced

3 sage leaves

2 teaspoons parsley, chopped

Nutmeg

780 ml (26 fl oz) Vegetable Stock (see page 36)

1 tablespoon single cream

Salt and black pepper to taste

Clean the leek well and coarsely chop. In a large pot, cook the shallot in the oil and butter over a medium heat until nearly transparent. Add the leek and continue to cook slowly until tender but without colour. Add the remaining vegetables, herbs, nutmeg and stock and simmer until the potato and pumpkin are tender and thoroughly cooked. Remove the sage.

Remove from the heat. Purée in batches in a blender until the soup is completely smooth. Pour the liquid through a sieve into a clean pot and stir in the single cream. Season with salt and pepper. Cover and set aside until ready to serve.

CROÛTONS

6 slices bread cut into 1 cm (½") cubes
2 tablespoons olive oil
Salt and pepper
1 tablespoon mixed chopped herbs (parsley, sage, thyme, rosemary)

———

Cut day-old bread into cubes and toss in olive oil, salt, pepper and herbs. Toast on a flat baking tray at Gas Mark 4/180°C/350°F for 5 minutes or until golden brown and crispy on the outside and soft in the middle.

ASSEMBLY

When ready to serve, heat the soups through and check the consistency of each. If one is too thick, add a small amount of stock until equal consistency is achieved. Scoop 125 ml (4 fl oz) of each into two equal-sized ladles. Holding one ladle in each hand, slowly pour out both soups at the same time, starting at the centre of the bowl. Move up and down for a straight line or play around with different designs. Serve immediately with croûtons on the side or on top of the soup. These soups are also delicious served chilled in the summertime.

ZUPPA REALE

This 'royal soup' is deliciously light and made from mixed vegetables and crispy egg-dough fritters.

Serves 6 (M) *35 minutes & 1 hour simmering*

STOCK

2 medium tomatoes

1 medium onion

2 medium courgettes

2 carrots

2 medium potatoes

2 branches celery

80 g (3 oz) spinach

2 garlic cloves

2 litres (4 pints) hot water

1 sprig parsley

1 teaspoon extra virgin olive oil

½ tablespoon sea salt

―――

Quarter the tomatoes and onion. Halve the courgettes, carrots, potatoes and celery and cut into large chunks. Combine all the ingredients. Cover and simmer for 1 hour. Strain and discard the vegetables.

FRITTATINE

4 whole eggs

6 tablespoons semolina

2 pinches salt

4 tablespoons grated Parmesan

Black pepper to taste

―――

Lightly beat all the ingredients together. One at a time, ladle 3 tablespoons of the egg mixture onto a buttered non-stick pan over a medium heat. Let the mixture spread to approximately 14 cm (5½") in diameter. When the bottom is cooked, gently flip with a spatula. Repeat with the remaining egg mix. Cut each fritter into 5 mm (¼") squares.

ESCAROLE

2 heads escarole, roughly chopped

2 garlic cloves

2 tablespooons extra virgin olive oil

Salt and pepper to taste

―――

Bring a large pot of lightly salted water to a boil. Flash the escarole in hot water for 1 minute then drain over a colander. Sauté the garlic in olive oil until golden brown, add the escarole and cook for another 1 minute. Season with salt and pepper.

ASSEMBLY

150 g (5 oz) Scamorza, or other soft mild cheese, cubed

―――

Heat the vegetable stock, add the escarole and Fritattine and simmer for 5 minutes. Divide the Scamorza between six bowls and ladle the soup over the cheese. Drizzle a few drops of olive oil on top and serve immediately.

PASTA e FAGIOLI

In the heat of the summer, fresh Borlotti beans and tomatoes are harvested at their peak. Best when made in July and August, this creamy and comforting stew with slightly under-ripe green bell peppers exudes the essence and flavours of an Italian kitchen garden. Serve with a smooth red wine, such as a dolcetto or merlot.

Serves 8   Ⓜ   *55 minutes & 1 hour simmering*

STEW

350 g (12½ oz) fresh Borlotti beans or 180 g (6 oz) dried beans previously soaked in water for 8 hours

6 basil leaves

2 parsley sprigs

4 garlic cloves

½ medium onion, sliced

1 celery stick

1 small green bell pepper, halved and deseeded

90 ml (3 fl oz) extra virgin olive oil

840 ml (28 fl oz) water

Salt to taste

3 peeled tomatoes, deseeded and roughly chopped

———

In a large saucepan, combine the beans with 3 basil leaves, 1 sprig of parsley, 2 cloves of garlic and half of the vegetables except the tomatoes. Add 3 tablespoons of olive oil, the water and 1 teaspoon of salt. Cover with a lid and cook slowly over a low heat until the beans are al dente, approximately 1 hour. Remove the vegetables with a slotted spoon, leaving only the beans and cooking liquid. In a separate saucepan, combine the tomatoes with the remaining ingredients. Cook over a low heat for 20 minutes until the liquid from the tomatoes has evaporated. Season with salt. Add the tomato the sauce to the beans and continue to cook over a low heat for 10 minutes. Remove the aromatic vegetables.

MALTAGLIATI

225 g (8 oz) Italian '00' flour

225 (8 oz) Grano Duro flour, plus more for dusting

1 tablespoon finely chopped herbs (thyme, sage and rosemary)

1 teaspoon extra virgin olive oil

Pinch of salt

225 ml (7¼ fl oz) water

———

Sift the flours together over a flat surface, add the herbs and make a well in the centre. Add the remaining ingredients and work into the flour with your fingers until a dough forms. Gather the dough into a ball and knead for 8 minutes until the texture is soft and elastic to the touch. Wrap in plastic film and rest for 15 minutes. Divide the dough in half and roll each portion into a long strip. Pass the dough halves through a pasta machine from the widest setting to number 6. Dry out for 10 minutes on a flat surface. Dust the surface of the pasta strips with Grano Duro flour and halve each strip vertically. Stack the four halves on top of each other and halve horizontally. Stack the eight quarters on top of each other and, starting from one corner, cut the dough into 1 cm (½") slices on a bias. Toss the pasta between your fingers to separate the pieces and lay them on a tray dusted with Grano Duro flour.

TO SERVE

Re-heat the bean stew. Bring a large pot of water to a boil. Season with salt and reduce to a simmer. Gently gather the pasta with your hands, shake off excess flour and cook in the boiling water. As soon as the pasta comes to the surface (approximately 1 minute), use a slotted spoon to transfer the pasta to the stew with beans. Gently stir the stew, taste for seasoning and serve immediately with a sprinkle of chopped basil and a drizzle of extra virgin olive oil over each portion.

Fresh pasta cooks much faster than dried, ready-made pasta.

ROTOLO di CRESPELLE

A roulade of crêpes stuffed with crunchy mixed vegetables. As delicious as it is beautiful, this dish is a huge success at any gathering. Great with a crisp white wine like a Müller Thurgau.

Serves 7 (M) *55 minutes*

CRÊPES

150 g (5 oz) flour
Salt and pepper to taste
250 ml (8½ fl oz) milk

3 eggs
1 tablespoon butter, melted

———

Put the flour, a pinch of salt and black pepper in a bowl. Whisk the milk, eggs and butter gently in another bowl. Add the liquid mixture to the dry one, whisking until even and clump-free. Set aside for 30 minutes. Heat a 23 cm (9") skillet or crêpe pan and brush lightly with butter. Remove the pan from the heat, ladle 60 ml (2 fl oz) of batter into the pan and swirl slowly to cover the base. Place back on the heat. When one side is golden brown, gently flip and cook the other side in the same manner. Repeat with the remaining batter. Set aside.

FILLING

3 garlic cloves
3 tablespoons chopped onion
3 sage leaves
3 mint leaves
1 tablespoon parsley, chopped
2 tablespoons butter
2 tablespoons extra virgin olive oil

700 g (1½ lb) julienned mixed vegetables,
    (courgettes, carrots and cabbage)
Salt and pepper to taste
2 egg yolks
6 oil-packed sundried tomatoes, chopped
50 g (1¾ oz) grated Parmesan
335 g (12 oz) ricotta
Nutmeg

———

Sauté the garlic, onion, sage, mint and parsley in the butter and olive oil over a medium heat. Cook until the onions are slightly transparent then add all the vegetables. Increase the heat to high and cook for 5 minutes, tossing occasionally. Season with salt and pepper. Remove from the heat, discard the garlic, sage and mint, and cool completely before mixing in the egg yolks, dried tomatoes, cheeses and nutmeg.

ASSEMBLY

½ tablespoon breadcrumbs mixed with 1 tablespoon grated Parmesan
3 tablespoons melted butter

———

Open three crêpes on a flat surface. Spread 2½ tablespoons of the vegetable mixture over each crêpe. Stack them on top of each other. From one end, gently roll the stack to create a large cannelloni shape. Set aside and continue with the remaining crêpes.

Slice the roulade into 2.5 cm (1½") slices. Place the pieces in a buttered casserole dish cut-side up. Spread the breadcrumbs over the surface and drizzle with melted butter. Cook at Gas Mark 4/180°C/350°F for 15 minutes or until the top is golden brown. Serve two slices per person.

This dish can be served with a variety of fillings. Feel free to experiment with your favourites.

A ravioli from the south Tyrol, on the Italian border with Austria. A spinach and potato dough ravioli stuffed with two mushroom varieties and topped with juniper cream and shallot sauces, a classic ravioli is transformed into the divine. Enjoy with a full bodied wine, such as an amarone.

Serves 5 **D** *80 minutes*

FILLING

150 g (5 oz) champignon and dry porcini
    mushrooms, roughly chopped
1 garlic clove, gently smashed
2 tablespoons extra virgin olive oil

Salt and pepper to taste
1 tablespoon chopped parsley
1 tablespoon grated Parmesan

———

Soak the dried porcini mushrooms in a small saucepan filled with hot water for 30 minutes. Drain through a colander. Sauté the garlic in the oil over a high heat. When it begins to colour, add all the mushrooms and cook until golden brown and the liquid has evaporated. Season with salt and pepper and cool before adding the parsley and Parmesan. Set aside.

SHALLOT SAUCE

3 shallots

75 ml (2½ fl oz) olive oil

———

With a mandolin, slice the shallots into thin rings. Caramelise in the oil over a low heat for 30 minutes or until dark and tender. Cover and set aside.

JUNIPER CREAM SAUCE

330 ml (11 fl oz) Vegetable Stock (see page 36)
5 juniper berries, crushed

1 tablespoon cornflour
210 ml (7 oz) single cream

———

Bring 125 ml (4 fl oz) of stock and the juniper berries to a boil to infuse for 5 minutes. Pass the stock through a sieve, discard the berries and add the infused stock to the regular stock. Heat to a simmer. Mix the cornflour with the cream and pour into the hot stock, whisking all the time. Continue whisking until the sauce comes to a simmer once more and cook for 1 more minute. Cover and set aside.

DOUGH

2 yellow potatoes
1 tablespoon butter
75 g (2½ oz) spinach, cooked and chopped
1 small egg, lightly beaten

Dash of nutmeg
Salt and pepper to taste
87 g (3 oz) Grano Duro flour

———

Boil and peel the potatoes. Mash with the butter while still hot. Cover and cool to room temperature. Place on a floured surface, add the finely chopped spinach and incorporate well. Add the egg, nutmeg, salt and pepper. Work the dough with a spatula to combine. Add the flour in three batches, incorporating well after each addition. Add more flour if the dough is still too sticky. Sprinkle the working surface with Grano Duro flour and roll a third of the dough into a large disc 2 mm (⅛") in thickness. Cut out as many circles as possible using a 5 cm (2") round cutter. Place ½ teaspoon of filling in the centre of each disc and close gently into a crescent shape. Seal by pressing lightly with your fingertips, leaving imprints. Continue with the remaining dough, reusing the scraps as well, until either the dough or the filling run out. Place the pieces, not touching, on a floured tray.

TO SERVE

Reheat both the shallot and the cream sauce, separately. Boil a pot of lightly salted water and reduce to a simmer. Gently add half the pasta to the water. When the ravioli rise to the surface, use a slotted spoon to transfer six pieces to each plate. Ladle over the cream sauce. Dot with shallots and shallot-infused oil. Repeat with the remaining pasta. Sprinkle with freshly ground white pepper and serve.

UMBRICELLI con SALSA di POMODORO, OLIVE e CAPPERI

A famous hand-rolled Umbrian pasta served with a tomato, caper and olive sauce. The texture and feel of the pasta can only be achieved by the use of hands, and the 'puttanesca'-like sauce demands the accompaniment of a merlot. Similar pasta is called 'Pici' in Tuscany.

Serves 5 Ⓜ *50 minutes*

DOUGH

180 g (6½ oz) Italian '00' flour
140 g (5 oz) Grano Duro flour
1 egg
125 ml (4 fl oz) water, at room temperature
½ teaspoon extra virgin olive oil
Pinch of salt

———

Sift both flours on to a flat work surface and make a well in the centre. Add the remaining ingredients to the well and work with your fingertips until a dough forms. Gather the dough and knead for 8 minutes. Wrap in plastic film and rest for 15 minutes.

Using a knife or pastry cutter, portion off a quarter of the dough, leaving the rest in the film. With a rolling pin, roll it into a long rectangle 5 mm (¼") thick. Cut into 5 mm (¼") wide strips starting from the short end. Roll each piece into a long, thin rope, approximately 3 mim (⅛") in diameter. Gently toss with dusting flour and transfer to a floured tray. Repeat with the remaining dough.

SAUCE

2 garlic cloves
2 tablespoons capers, roughly chopped
12 black olives, roughly chopped
4 tablespoons extra virgin olive oil
1½ quantities Tomato Sauce (see page 36)
1 handful grated Parmesan

TO SERVE

Bring a large pot of lightly salted water to a boil and reduce to a simmer. In a separate pan, sauté the garlic, capers and olives in the olive oil until the garlic is golden brown. Remove the garlic, add the Tomato Sauce and heat. Slide the pasta into the simmering water. Refrain from stirring the delicate noodles; if pieces stick together as they come to the surface, gently separate with a fork. Cook for an additional minute after the pasta comes to the surface and check for doneness. When al dente, drain off the water, reserving 250 ml (8 fl oz) of cooking liquid, and add the pasta and Parmesan to the sauce. Toss together, adding the reserved cooking liquid if too dry. Serve immediately.

RISOTTO allo ZAFFERANO

The comforting texture and sophisticated flavour of this saffron risotto make this one of the most praised dishes at the Country House Montali. Pair with a mild white wine, like regaleali or sauvignon blanc, so to not interfere with the saffron.

Serves 5 Ⓔ *20 minutes & 1 hour soaking*

INGREDIENTS

1 teaspoons saffron threads

300 g (11 oz) uncooked rice, Carnaroli or Arborio

750 ml (25 fl oz) Vegetable Stock (see page 36)

1 tablespoon extra virgin olive oil

2 tablespoons butter

1 small garlic clove, minced

½ medium onion, finely chopped

80 ml (2 ½ fl oz) white wine

100 g (3½ oz) Fontina or Taleggio, cut into 5 mm (½") cubes

6 tablespoons grated Parmigiano Reggiano

Salt and white pepper to taste

———

Soak the saffron in 3 tablespoons of hot water for 1 hour. Rinse the rice thoroughly and drain. Heat the stock in a saucepan until it just comes to a boil and turn off the heat.

In another medium saucepan, heat olive the oil and half the butter together over a medium-low heat. When the butter has melted, add the garlic and onion and cook slowly, stirring. When the onion is translucent, add the rice and stir. When the rice becomes slightly translucent, add the white wine and stir until evaporated. Add the hot stock, two ladles at a time, stirring gently until the liquid nearly evaporates before each addition.

Add the saffron and its soaking water into the risotto and stir to combine. If the rice is still undercooked, add a small amount of hot water. When the rice is al dente (about 15 minutes from the start of cooking), turn off the heat and stir in the cheeses and remaining butter. Season to taste with salt and white pepper and serve immediately.

When using the parboiled variety, rice will usually take 12 to 15 minutes to cook. For best results, check instructions for each brand of rice.

FRANCOBOLLI di GORGONZOLA al PESTO

Rich, decorative francobolli, or 'stamps', are stuffed with rich Gorgonzola cheese and served with a classic pesto sauce. Pair with a strong red wine. Pesto is surely one of the greatest achievements of the city of Genoa, from where it originates.

Serves 8 **D** *35 minutes*

DOUGH

150 g (5½ oz) Italian '00' flour

100 g (3½ oz) Grano Duro flour, plus more for dusting

2 whole eggs

3 egg yolks

Pinch of salt

½ teaspoon extra virgin olive oil

———

Sift the flours on to a flat work surface and create a well in the centre. Add the remaining ingredients to the well and work with your fingertips until the dough comes together. Gather into a ball and knead for 3 minutes. If the dough feels dry, moisten your hands with water and continue to work. Cover with plastic film and refrigerate for 15 minutes.

FILLING

55 g (2 oz) Crescenza or creamy goat's cheese

90 g (3 oz) Gorgonzola

———

Beat both cheeses together with a fork until very creamy and transfer to a piping bag with a 7 mm (⅜") tip. Refrigerate for at least 15 minutes to keep firm.

SAUCE

½ quantity Pesto (see page 31)

1 teaspoon butter

Grated Parmesan

Black pepper to taste

ASSEMBLY

1 egg white, lightly beaten, for brushing

———

Roll the dough to number 7 through a pasta mill into a long sheet approximately 14 cm (5½") wide. Brush one half of the pasta with the egg white. Leaving a 1 cm (½") border around the edges, pipe out approximately ⅓ teaspoonfuls of cheese filling 2 cm (¾") apart over the brushed half (see picture). Carefully cover with the unbrushed half and press gently between the columns of filling to seal. Press around each ball of filling with your fingertips to push out excess air. Trim the outside borders with a ribbed pasta cutter, then run the cutter through first the columns then the rows of the francobolli to separate each piece. Place the pasta, not touching, on a floured tray.

In a medium sauté pan, heat the Pesto with the butter until warm. Bring a pot of lightly salted water to a boil and reduce to a simmer. Slide the pasta from the tray into the simmering water to cook, avoiding the addition of dusting flour into the water. As soon as the pasta comes to the surface, transfer with a slotted spoon directly into the Pesto. Add ½ ladleful of the pasta cooking liquid. Toss the pasta three or four times so that each piece of pasta is coated with pesto and transfer to a large serving dish. Sprinkle with grated Parmesan and black pepper and serve immediately.

STROGANOFF

A meatless version of a popular Russian recipe, this vegetarian variety loses none of the famous texture or flavour with the addition of seitan. Savour on a cold winter night with a glass of hearty barbaresco wine.

Serves 6 (M) *50 minutes*

SAUCE

3 garlic cloves, 2 whole and 1 minced

5 tablespoons extra virgin olive oil

450 g (1 lb) porcini or button mushrooms, sliced

½ quantity Seitan (see page 35)

1 shallot, finely chopped

2 tablespoons butter

3 tablespoons brandy or cognac

1½ quantity Tomato Sauce (see page 36)

200 ml (6½ fl oz) single cream

———

Sauté 2 whole garlic cloves in 3 tablespoons olive oil over a high heat. Add the mushrooms when the garlic begins to colour and cook until they are browned and the liquid has evaporated. Take out the garlic (you can throw it away) and set aside the mushrooms. Slice the seitan into 1 x 4 cm (½ x 1½") pieces. Sauté the minced garlic and shallot in the remaining olive oil and butter for 1 minute over a medium heat. Add the Seitan and cook for 5 minutes or until nicely browned. Flambé with alcohol (see page 21). Add the mushrooms to the Seitan and cook for an additional minute. Heat the Tomato Sauce to a simmer, mix in the single cream and add the seitan-mushroom mixture. Stir well to combine the ingredients. Cover and set aside.

RICE

550 ml (18⅓ fl oz) Vegetable Stock (see page 36)

1 small garlic clove, minced

1 small shallot, finely chopped

1 tablespoon extra virgin olive oil

1 tablespoon butter

300 g (10½ oz) parboiled rice, rinsed

Salt and pepper to taste

———

Bring the stock to a simmer. In a large heavy-bottomed pot, gently sauté the garlic and shallot in olive oil and butter until translucent. Stir in the rice and cook for 1 minute. Add the stock, cover with a lid and cook over a low heat for 12 minutes, or until the rice has absorbed all the liquid and is cooked. Reheat the sauce and serve surrounding the rice on individual plates.

CANNELLONI di RICOTTA con SUGO di POMODORO

Ricotta cheese cannelloni with tomato sauce. An Italian family favourite for Sunday lunch, this classic cannelloni needs only a simple tomato sauce and glass of mild red wine.

Serves 6 Ⓜ *45 minutes*

DOUGH

165 g (6 oz) Italian '00' flour
85 g (3 oz) Grano Duro flour, plus more for dusting
2 whole eggs

3 egg yolks
1 pinch salt
1 teaspoon extra virgin olive oil

———

Sift the flours together on a flat surface and make a well in the centre. In a separate bowl, lightly beat the remaining ingredients together and add to the well. Work with your fingertips until a dough forms. Gather the dough and knead well for 5 minutes until the texture is smooth and elastic. Wrap in plastic film and rest for 15 minutes. Cut the dough in three, roll each portion to number 6 through a pasta mill and lay out on a floured surface. Cut into 12 cm (5") squares and layer between parchment paper dusted with Grano Duro flour. Bring a large pot of lightly salted water to a boil and reduce to a simmer. Prepare an ice bath with a tablespoon of oil. Cook the pasta in batches of eight, adding to the water one at a time. As soon as each square comes to the surface, transfer to the ice bath with a slotted spoon to cool quickly. Transfer the pasta one by one on to a clean, dry towel on a flat surface. Do not overlap the squares.

FILLING

336 g (12 oz) fresh ricotta
1 egg
Black pepper to taste
Nutmeg

1 tablespoon grated Pecorino Romano
1 tablespoon grated Parmigiano Reggiano
1 tablespoon grated Pecorino di Pienza
Zest of ½ lemon

———

Beat the ricotta with a fork until creamy. Add the remaining ingredients and mix until smooth. Set aside.

SUGO DI POMODORO

2 garlic cloves, peeled
3 tablespoons extra virgin olive oil
½ tablespoon chopped parsley

½ tablespoon chopped basil
1½ quantity Tomato Sauce (see page 36), warmed

———

Sauté the garlic in olive oil until coloured, then discard. Add the herbs to the oil, stir to infuse, then add to the warm Tomato Sauce. Set aside.

ASSEMBLY

60 g (2 oz) grated Parmigiano Reggiano

224 g (8 oz) mozzarella, cut into
5 mm (¼") cubes

———

Using a piping bag or spoon, place 2 tablespoons of filling on one edge of each pasta square and roll up evenly so that each cannelloni is 2 cm (¾") thick. Ladle half the sauce onto the bottom of a medium casserole pan, spreading evenly. Line the cannelloni over the sauce. Sprinkle with Parmigiano Reggiano, cover with the remainder of the sugo sauce, then top with mozzarella. Bake at Gas Mark 4/180°C/350°F for 13 minutes. Serve immediately.

SPAGHETTI alla CHITARRA con SALSA ai QUATTRO FORMAGGI e TARTUFO

This famous guitar string spaghetti is for all rock 'n' roll aficionados! Cut from a guitar-like pasta cutter, this dish features three different kinds of pasta and is served with Four Cheese and Truffle sauces.

Serves 4 **D** *75 minutes*

SAFFRON DOUGH

70 g (2½ oz) Italian '00' flour

70 g (2½ oz) Grano Duro flour

1 whole egg

2 egg yolks

Pinch of salt

½ teaspoon extra virgin olive oil

½ teaspoon saffron powder*

*If using saffron powder, soak in 2 tablespoons hot water for one hour. Add an additional tablespoon of Italian '00' flour to the dough when mixing.

SPINACH DOUGH

55 g (2 oz) Italian '00' flour

55 g (2 oz) Grano Duro flour

30 g (1 oz) cooked spinach, squeezed and puréed

1 whole egg

1 egg yolk

Pinch of salt

½ teaspoon extra virgin olive oil

BEETROOT DOUGH

55 g (2 oz) Italian '00' flour

55 g (2 oz) Grano Duro flour

30 g (1 oz) beetroot, peeled, steamed and puréed*

1 egg yolk and 1 whole egg

Pinch of salt

½ teaspoon extra virgin olive oil

*Make sure you drain the puréed beetroot of excess water.

Starting with the Saffron Dough, sift the flours on to a flat surface and make a well in the centre. Add the remaining dough ingredients into the well and work with your fingertips until a ball forms. Knead for 3 minutes. Roll into a ball, cover with plastic film and set aside. Repeat this process for the Spinach and Beetroot doughs.

Start with one ball of dough. Roll out half the dough into a 5 x 20 cm (2 x 8") rectangle, 2 mm (⅛") thick, over a flat surface dusted with Grano Duro flour. Repeat with the other doughs and dry over a floured tray for 10 minutes. Cut with either a pasta guitar, pressing the dough through the strings with a rolling pin, or with a long knife. If using a knife, flour each strip and wrap around a rolling pin starting from the short end. Carefully slide out the rolling pin and cut the roll crosswise into 2 mm (⅛") wide strips. Toss with Grano Duro flour and set, in nests, on a floured tray.

SAUCE

Four Cheese Sauce (see page 28)

1 quantity Sage Butter (see page 32)

1 quantity Truffle Sauce (see page 36)

Heat the Four Cheese Sauce in a double boiler. Bring a pot of salted water to a boil and reduce to a simmer. Cook the pastas together in the pot. As soon as they come to the surface, remove from the heat and drain through a colander. In a large non-stick sauté pan, melt the Sage Butter, add the pasta and toss together. Pour the Cheese Sauce on to individual plates and add the pasta. Drizzle with more Cheese Sauce and dot with Truffle Sauce.

MACCHERONI LADUS

Of Sardinian origin, this 'stretched maccheroni' is a handmade pasta served with a medley of earthy vegetables in a tomato sauce. Wonderful with a Sardinian 'cannonau' or a pinot noir.

Serves 6 Ⓜ *60 minutes*

MACCHERONI DOUGH

154 g (5½ oz) Italian '00' flour
140 g (5 oz) Grano Duro flour
1 egg

90 ml (3 fl oz) water, at room temperature
½ teaspoon extra virgin olive oil
1 pinch of salt

———

Sift both flours on to a flat work surface and make a well in the centre. Add the remaining ingredients to the well and work with your fingertips until a dough forms. Gather the dough and knead for 8 minutes. Wrap in plastic film and rest for 15 minutes.

Using a knife or pastry cutter, portion off a quarter of the dough, leaving the rest in the film, and roll out into a long rope 5 mm (⅓") thick over a floured surface. Cut the rope into 5 mm (⅓") pieces. Roll each piece into a ball, press the middle with your thumb, and gently push forward to pull the dough. With your fingertips, gently stretch each piece into a 5 x 2 cm (2 x ¾") rough rectangle. Transfer the pasta to a floured tray and repeat with the remaining dough.

STEW

1 small red bell pepper
1 aubergine, peeled and cubed
3 courgettes, cubed
Vegetable oil, for deep frying
1 tablespoon parsley

2 garlic cloves, minced
3 tablespoons extra virgin olive oil
5 tomatoes, peeled, cubed and deseeded
250 ml (8 fl oz) Vegetable Stock
   (see page 36)

———

Blacken and peel the bell pepper (see page 20) and cut into 4 x 1 cm (1½ x ½") pieces. In batches, deep-fry both the aubergine and courgette cubes until brown. Transfer from the hot oil to a tray lined with paper towels. Season and allow to cool to room temperature. Cook the parsley and garlic in the olive oil for 1 minute, drop in the tomatoes and cook for 10 minutes. Add the aubergine, courgettes and red pepper and cook for 3 minutes before adding the hot stock. Cook for an additional minute.

TO SERVE

Grated Pecorino Pienza

———

Bring a pot of salted water to a boil. Reduce to a simmer, and slide in the pasta from tray. Cook to al dente (approximately 5 minutes), drain off the cooking liquid and transfer the pasta to the stew. Add a handful of grated cheese and serve immediately.

GNOCCHI di PATATE

The soft, mouth-watering texture of this famous potato pasta makes gnocchi one of the most frequently demanded dishes in Italy. The quick flick of the fingers in the preparation of the pasta adds to the enjoyment of making gnocchi at home. Choose a strong red wine to accompany the Four Cheese Sauce.

Serves 4 (M) *35 minutes*

DOUGH

4 medium potatoes, yellow or red

¼ tablespoon butter

1 pinch salt

1 pinch nutmeg

2 egg yolks

70 g (2½ oz) Italian '00' flour

70 g (2½ oz) Grano Duro flour, plus more for dusting

———

Cook and peel the potatoes. Push through a potato ricer onto a lightly floured surface and add the butter and salt. Work well with a spatula until evenly incorporated. Cover and cool completely. Add the nutmeg and egg yolks and work them into the potato with your hands until the dough is even in colour and texture. In batches, incorporate the two flours into the dough with the help of a pastry cutter. When the dough begins to come together, knead quickly and gently until even, adding more Grano Duro if too sticky.

Using a pastry cutter or knife, portion off 2 tablespoons of dough. Roll out on a lightly floured surface into a long 1 cm (½") thick rope. Cut into 1 cm (½") pieces. Gently press your index and middle fingers into the centre of one piece and slowly roll your fingers back towards you, allowing the dough to follow and form a shell shape. Repeat with the remaining dough, gently tossing batches with Grano Duro flour to avoid sticking. Set aside on a floured tray, making sure the pieces do not touch.

SAUCE/GARNISH

1 handful grapes

Icing sugar, for sprinkling

½ handful chopped walnuts

1 quantity Four Cheese Sauce

(see page 28)

———

Peel and halve the grapes. Gently remove the seeds and lay the halves, face-down, over a sheet of parchment paper. Barely sprinkle with icing sugar and bake at Gas Mark 4/180°C/350°F for 10 minutes. Heat the Four Cheese Sauce over a double boiler and transfer to a sauté pan.

ASSEMBLY

Bring a pot of lightly salted water to a simmer and slide the gnocchi from the tray. As soon as the pieces come to the surface (approximately 1 minute), remove with a slotted spoon and place immediately into the sauce. Toss together and transfer to a large serving platter or individual plates. Garnish with chopped walnuts and baked grape halves and serve immediately.

RISO alla ORIENTALE

An aromatic basmati rice served with a lively tomato sauce laden with peas, oriental spices and paneer, a homemade cheese. Enjoy this interesting combination of flavours with a crisp gewürztraminer wine.

Serves 5 Ⓜ *70 minutes*

PANEER

1 quantity Paneer (see page 30)

2 tablespoons Ghee (see page 28)

Salt and black pepper to taste

———

Cut the Paneer into 1 x 1 cm (½ x ½") pieces. Sauté in ghee until golden brown and season to taste.

SAUCE

200 g (7 oz) peas

4 tablespoons extra virgin olive oil

½ small onion, sliced

1 teaspoon cumin seeds

1 shallot, chopped

1 small garlic clove, minced

2 tablespoons Ghee (see page 28)

1 tablespoon grated ginger

1 small green bell pepper, deseeded and chopped

10 tomatoes, depeeled, seeded and chopped

1 teaspoon ground coriander

1 teaspoon curry powder

1 teaspoon ground fennel seeds

1 tablespoon brown sugar

1 tablespoon mint, chopped

2 tablespoons parsley, chopped

180 ml (6 fl oz) plain yoghurt, at room temperature

Salt and black pepper to taste

———

Combine the peas with 1 tablespoon olive oil, onion, salt, black pepper and enough water to cover. Cook until the peas are tender. Drain the liquid off and discard the onion. Heat the cumin seeds, shallot and garlic in 2 tablespoons olive oil and 2 tablespoons ghee until the cumin seeds colour. Add the ginger and green pepper and roast for 1 minute. Add the tomatoes, coriander, curry powder, fennel, sugar and half the fresh herbs. Cook for 15 minutes partly covered, stirring occasionally. Purée in a blender, transfer back to the heat, add the peas and cook for 5 minutes. Remove from the heat, cool for 10 minutes, and slowly mix in the yoghurt until fully combined. Add the Paneer and remaining herbs and taste for seasoning. Keep warm.

RICE

3 tablespoons sesame seeds

Salt

345 ml (12 fl oz) Vegetable Stock (see page 36)

1 small garlic clove

2 shallots, finely chopped

2 tablespoons olive oil

2 tablespoons butter

210 g (7½ oz) Basmati or long grain rice

2 tablespoons melted Ghee (see page 28)

2 tablespoons chopped parsley

———

Toast the sesame seeds in ½ teaspoon of salt and set aside. Heat the stock and keep at a simmer. In a heavy-bottomed pot, gently sauté the garlic and shallots in the olive oil and butter until the shallots are transparent. Stir in the rice and cook for 1 minute. Add the stock, partly cover with a lid and cook over a low heat for 10 minutes, or until the rice has absorbed all the liquid and is cooked. Divide the rice between six serving plates, drizzle with Ghee and sprinkle with parsley and the sesame seeds. Serve alongside the sauce.

GNOCCHETTI SARDI

These small Sardinian gnocchi are made from durum wheat flour. While the shape of this pasta is similar to that of the Gnocchi di Patate, the texture and sauce of this spectacular Mediterranean dish capture the essence of a refreshing Italian summer.

Serves 6 ⓂⓂ *40 minutes & 1 hour resting*

TOMATO OLIVE SAUCE

600 g (1 lb 5oz) cherry tomatoes, deseeded, cut into eighths

70 g (2½ oz) black olives, roughly chopped

70 g (2½ oz) green olives, roughly chopped

14 g (½ oz) capers

5 basil leaves

1 whole garlic clove, puréed

1 teaspoon oregano

1 tablespoon chopped parsley

Salt and black pepper to taste

1 teaspoon soy sauce

6 tablespoons extra virgin olive oil

1 small courgette, grated

———

Combine all ingredients in a large bowl and squeeze with your hands to mix together and break up the tomatoes. Cover and set aside for 1 hour for the flavours to combine.

DOUGH

154 g (5½ oz) Italian '00' flour

140 g (5 oz) Grano Duro flour

1 egg

125 ml (4 fl oz) water, room temperature

½ teaspoon extra virgin olive oil

Pinch of salt

———

Sift both flours on to a flat work surface and make a well in the centre. Add the remaining ingredients to the well and work with your fingertips until a dough forms. Gather the dough and knead for 8 minutes. Wrap in plastic film and rest for 15 minutes.

Using a knife or pastry cutter, portion off a quarter of the dough, leaving the rest in the film, and roll out into a long rope 1 cm (½") thick over a floured surface. Cut the rope into 1 cm (½") pieces. Press each piece in the middle with the tip of a thumb and gently roll forward, creating a shell-like shape. Repeat with the remaining dough and transfer the pasta to a floured tray.

TO SERVE

60 g (2 oz) Pecorino di Pienza, cut into small cubes

280 g (10 oz) buffalo mozzarella for topping

5 basil leaves

Chilli oil, optional

———

Add the Pecorino di Pienza to the Tomato Olive Sauce. Bring a large pot of lightly salted water to a boil and reduce to a simmer. Shake off the excess flour from the gnocchetti through a colander and add the pasta to the cooking water. When the pasta comes to the surface, cook for an additional minute or until al dente. Drain off the water and add the hot pasta to the sauce. Toss to combine and serve immediately, topped with mozzarella, freshly chopped basil and a drizzle of chilli oil if desired.

GNOCCHI alla ROMANA

This variety of gnocchi originates from Rome, where the semolina pasta is cut into discs, layered, then baked with a topping of juniper sauce and grated cheese. Take pleasure in this hearty winter dish with a good sangiovese wine.

Serves 6　Ⓜ　*50 minutes*

GNOCCHI

1 litre (1¾ pints) milk

70 g (2½ oz) butter, plus more for greasing

210 g (7½ oz) semolina

Pinch of nutmeg

Salt and black pepper to taste

28 g (1 oz) grated Pecorino Romano

60 g (2 oz) grated Parmesan

1 egg yolk, beaten

———

Combine the milk and butter in a saucepan and bring to a boil. Add the semolina and cook for 20 minutes stirring continuously. Mix in the nutmeg, salt, pepper, Pecorino Romano and half the grated Parmesan. Remove from the heat and stir for 1 minute to cool slightly before adding in the egg yolk. Pour the dough on to a buttered marble or granite surface and, using wet hands, flatten it out into a large rectangle. Dampen a rolling pin and roll the dough out into a 25 x 43 cm (10 x 17") rectangle that is 5 mm (¼") thick. Wet the rim of a 5 cm (2") glass cup and cut out as many round discs from the dough as possible. Butter an 20 x 28 cm (8 x 11") baking dish and line the bottom with the dough trimmings. Overlap the discs over the trimmings, sprinkle the surface with the remaining grated Parmesan and dot with butter.

A large cutting board covered with buttered parchment paper may replace a marble or granite surface.

SAUCE

500 ml (16 fl oz) Vegetable Stock (see page 36)

5 juniper berries, crushed or finely chopped

1 tablespoon cornflour

300 ml (10 fl oz) single cream

1 handful grated Parmesan

White pepper

———

Combine the ingredients (without the Parmesan) in a saucepan, mix well and bring to a boil. Add the Parmesan and cook, stirring until the cheese has melted. Set aside.

TO SERVE

Bake the gnocchi at Gas Mark4/180°C/350°F for 15 minutes or until golden brown. Heat the sauce, ladle over the gnocchi and serve hot with a sprinkle of white pepper.

CAPPELLETTI al POMODORO

This unique ravioli stuffing of roasted peppers, sheep's cheese and spinach makes for a delectable and impressive pasta dish worth every bit of the effort.

Serves 5   (M)   *50 minutes*

DOUGH

150 g (5½ oz) Italian '00' Flour

50 g (1¾ oz) Grano Duro flour, plus more for dusting

3 egg yolks

1 whole egg

Pinch of salt

½ teaspoon extra virgin olive oil

2 teaspoons tomato paste

———

Sift the flours onto a flat work surface and create a well in the centre. Add the remaining ingredients to the well and work with your fingertips until the dough comes together. Knead for 3 minutes. If the dough feels very dry, wet your hands and continue to work. Cover with plastic film and refrigerate for 30 minutes.

FILLING

½ small red bell pepper

2 cloves garlic, 1 whole and 1 sliced thinly

½ tablespoon chopped celery

Salt and black pepper to taste

Extra virgin olive oil

55 g (2 oz) cooked spinach, squeezed

28 g (1 oz) Pecorino cheese, grated

1 egg white, lightly beaten

42 g (1½ oz) brie, cut into
   5 mm (¼") cubes

———

Blacken the bell pepper (see page 20) and cut into 1 cm (½") squares. Toss with the sliced garlic, celery, salt, pepper and olive oil to coat. Meanwhile, sauté the whole garlic clove in olive oil until golden brown. Add the spinach and cook for 2 minutes, seasoning to taste. Remove from the heat and cool. Mix the grated cheese with 1 tablespoon of egg white to form a paste. Reserve the remaining egg white for brushing.

ASSEMBLY AND SERVE

2 quantities Tomato Sauce (see page 36)

1 handful basil leaves, roughly chopped

Parmigiano Reggiano for topping

———

Roll out the dough to number 7 through a pasta mill and, over a flat surface dusted with Grano Duro, cut into circles using a 10 cm (4") round cutter. Brush half the surface with egg white. Place a pinch of spinach slightly off the centre of each disc. Top with one piece of brie, pepper and a pinch of the grated cheese paste. Close the un-brushed side over the filling into a crescent shape and seal by gently pushing out the air from the centre. Wrap the ends of the crescent around and close together. Line the cappelletti on a tray dusted with Grano Duro flour.

Heat the Tomato Sauce in a large sauté pan with the basil. Bring a pot of lightly salted water to a boil and reduce to a simmer. Slide the cappelletti into the water and cook until the pasta rises to surface and floats for about 3 minutes. Transfer with a slotted spoon into the sauce and toss briefly to combine. Serve with a drizzle of olive oil and shavings of Parmigiano Reggiano to taste.

PIZZOCCHERI

A speciality of Valtellina in the Italian Alps, this pasta is made partly with buckwheat flour, creating a highly unusual texture. Match the beautifully blended flavours of cabbage and spinach with a full-bodied wine like an amarone or cabernet sauvignon.

Serves 8 Ⓜ *45 minutes*

DOUGH

400 g (14 oz) Grano Duro flour, plus more for dusting
200 g (7 oz) buckwheat flour
4 eggs, lightly beaten
2 tablespoons Grappa liquor
6 tablespoons beer
Pinch of salt

———

Combine both flours on a flat surface and make a well in the centre. Add the remaining ingredients to the well and work with your fingers until a dough forms. Gather into a ball and knead well for 8 minutes. Wrap in plastic film and refrigerate for 30 minutes. Then roll out to number 6 through a pasta mill into a long strip, or by hand into a large wafer-thin disc. Dry, uncovered, for 10 minutes.

If rolling out through a pasta mill, halve vertically and horizontally, flour the surface and stack the quarters. Slice into 1 cm (½") strips. If rolling out by hand, dust the surface with Grano Duro flour and roll the dough over a rolling pin from the bottom up until all the dough is wrapped around the pin. Take a sharp knife and cut lengthwise across the top of the pin in a straight line and let the dough fall away. Remove the pin and cut again lengthwise across the middle. Dust the surface of one stack with flour and place the two stacks on top of each other. Cut crosswise into 1 cm (½") strips. Gently toss pieces with more flour and set aside on a floured tray.

SAUCE

3 garlic cloves, gently smashed
3 sage leaves
170 g (6 oz) butter
2 medium potatoes, peeled and cut into 1 cm (½") cubes
300 g (11 oz) savoy cabbage, spinach, or black cabbage, roughly julienned
200 g (7 oz) mildly aged cheese like Fontina or Gouda, cut into small cubes
100 g (3½ oz) grated Parmesan
White pepper

———

Heat the garlic and sage with the butter in a small sauté pan. When the garlic begins to colour, press the cloves down with the back of a spoon to extract the juices, then discard the cloves. Set aside the butter with sage. Cook the potatoes and greens in 2 litres (3½ pints) of lightly salted simmering water for 10 minutes. Slide the pasta from the tray and cook for an additional 5 minutes (the pasta should be slightly undercooked). Drain water from the pasta and vegetables. Spread half of the pasta mixture and half of the sage butter sauce over the bottom of a 23 x 33 cm (9 x 13") casserole dish. Top with half of the cubed cheese and half the grated Parmesan. Repeat the procedure. Sprinkle with the remaining Parmesan and bake at Gas Mark 4/180°C/350°F for 10–15 minutes. Top with a sprinkle of freshly ground white pepper and serve in the casserole dish.

TIMBALLO alla TERAMANA

Originally from the town of Teramo in central Italy, this timballo is constructed of five layers of crespelle (thin crêpes) and four succulently prepared vegetables. Serve this impressive dish on special occasions with a sauvignon blanc or a vermentino di sardegna.

Serves 6 **D** *90 minutes*

CRÊPES

250 ml (8 fl oz) milk

100 g (3½ oz) flour

28 g (1 oz) butter, plus more for cooking

1 egg

Salt and pepper to taste

———

Whisk the ingredients together. Heat a non-stick 20 cm (8") skillet or crêpe pan over a medium-high heat. Spread 1 teaspoon of butter around the pan and wipe with a paper towel. Remove the pan from the heat. Ladle 50 ml (2 fl oz) of batter into the pan and swirl to spread. Place the pan back on the heat and cook until one side is golden. Flip and cook the other side. Repeat with the remaining batter (makes 12 crêpes).

FILLING

3 garlic cloves

1 sprig rosemary

7 tablespoons extra virgin olive oil

250 g (9 oz) mushrooms, roughly chopped

Salt, black pepper and white pepper to taste

200 g (7 oz) peas

2 shallots, chopped

280 g (10 oz) courgettes, cut into
   1 cm (½") cubes

250 g (9 oz) cooked spinach

7 g (¼ oz) butter

100 g (3½ oz) grated Parmesan

30 g (1 oz) grated Pecorino Romano

250 g (9 oz) mozzarella, cut into
   1 cm (½") cubes

———

Mushrooms: Sauté 2 cloves of garlic and the rosemary in 2 tablespoons of olive oil until brown. Add the mushrooms and sauté over a high heat. Cook until the liquid has evaporated. Remove from the heat, take out the garlic and rosemary and season to taste. Set aside.

Peas: Cook the peas, half the chopped shallots, 1½ tablespoons of olive oil, white pepper and enough water to just cover. When the peas are tender, remove the vegetables, strain off the liquid, season to taste and set aside.

Courgettes: Sauté the courgettes with the remaining shallots in 1½ tablespoons of olive oil. Cook until any liquid has evaporated and season to taste. Remove from the heat and set aside.

Spinach: Sauté the spinach in the butter, remaining oil and garlic. Season to taste. Remove from the heat and discard the garlic. Chop well and set aside.

ASSEMBLY

Grease a 20 cm (8") square baking dish. Line the bottom with two crêpes. Sprinkle with a quarter of each grated cheese. Spread the chopped spinach over the bottom. Add a quarter of the mozzarella cubes over the spinach. Line with two more crêpes. Repeat this process of crêpes, grated cheese, vegetables and mozzarella with the mushrooms, peas and then courgettes. Top the final layer with the remaining two crêpes. Dot with butter. Cover with aluminium foil and bake at Gas Mark 4/180°C/350°F for 20 minutes. Remove from the heat. Using clean scissors, cut into six equal portions. Serve immediately.

RISOTTO allo ZENZERO e LIMONE

This ginger and lemon risotto is, as some put it, mystifyingly good. One of the most celebrated risottos in Montali. Pair with a flowery white wine, like a gewürztraminer, and never with a red.

Serves 4   **E**   *20 minutes*

INGREDIENTS

½ small onion, finely chopped

1 shallot, finely chopped

1 small garlic clove, minced

1 sage leaf

3 tablespoons extra virgin olive oil

250 g (9 oz) pumpkin, peeled and cut into 2.5 cm (1") pieces

125 ml (4¼ fl oz) water

Salt and white pepper to taste

280 g (10 oz) Carnaroli or Arborio rice

530 ml (17½ fl oz) Vegetable Stock (see page 36)

75 ml (2½ fl oz) white wine

½ tablespoon ginger, peeled and grated

1 tablespoon parsley, finely chopped

1 tablespoon butter

4 tablespoons grated Parmigiano Reggiano

2 tablespoons lemon juice

SAUCE

In a large pot, cook half the chopped onion, shallot and the garlic and the sage in 2 tablespoons of olive oil over a medium-low heat. When the vegetables are translucent, add the pumpkin and water. Cover and cook until the squash is tender. Discard the sage and mash the pumpkin mixture with a fork. Season to taste with salt and white pepper. Cover and set aside.

RICE

Rinse and drain the rice. In a small pot, bring the stock to a boil then turn off the heat. In a separate pot, heat the remaining oil over a medium heat with the remaining chopped onion, shallot and garlic, cooking until the onion and shallot are translucent. Add the rice, cooking until the rice is slightly transparent. Add the white wine and stir gently for 30 seconds. Add the stock two ladles at a time, stirring in a gentle wave-like motion and allowing the rice to absorb the stock before each addition. When the rice is half-cooked (about 7 minutes after the start of cooking), mix in the ginger, pumpkin and ½ tablespoon parsley. Continue to add ladles of stock until the rice is al dente (about 7 additional minutes). Take off the heat and add the butter, 2 tablespoons of grated Parmigiano Reggiano and the lemon juice, mixing well. Season to taste and serve with a sprinkle of remaining grated cheese and parsley.

need discipline in this life because in this job you are always 'on stage' somehow.

I still remember my first big 'lesson of discipline' when I assisted in my own kitchen more then 20 years ago. I already mentioned my best chef, Akira Shishido from Japan. He worked hard for us for two full years alone in the kitchen. After two years, we decided to hire another Japanese chef to help him.

Of course, it didn't work: Akira was the Schumacher of the situation and he was simply, constantly, training himself to be better in the kitchen. The young sous chef was just a cook without the love and self-denial required for this job, even though he was a nice chap.

And they were both Japanese – so different from us Italians!!

One afternoon I arrived in my restaurant at about 5.00 pm. The chefs usually arrived at 4.00 pm and started to prepare the food for the restaurant, which would open at 8.00 pm. Of course, I was expecting to find Masa (the sous chef) working in the kitchen with Akira. But my major surprise was that I found him standing on the doorstep of the kitchen. Seeing his face, I immediately understood that he had not gone out to smoke a cigarette or to relax a minute. His eyes were watching his shoes, with the typical guilty face that the Japanese put on when their boss is ready to ask them to commit suicide on the spot. Of course, as a 'white monkey' myself (that is what they called us sometimes), I wasn't particularly keen on entering a situation which wasn't promising to be either friendly or easy, particularly between two Orientals.

Unfortunately I was the boss, and this was my restaurant. So, with politeness, I had to try to understand what had just happened. It was the usual situation in which the executive-chef (Akira) had not liked one of the mistakes the sous chef Masa had just made, for the sixth time that day!! God's heaven, Akira got mad, and, as he didn't manage to obtain an instant hara-kiri from Masa (in Italy it would have been inappropriate), he imposed on the young one the punishment of having to stand on the doorstep without moving for the whole night!

That was for him the minimum punishment for someone who had just burnt the risotto for the third time. In my imagination, I caught just a quick glimpse of the titles in the Italian newspapers if I ever dared to do something like this to any of my employees!! The unions would have surely deep-fried me on the burner with lots of boiling olive oil and rosemary. (Let's not say where they would have put the carrot.) Of course, I bet the Japanese unions were more than happy not to be involved in all the blood of a hara-kiri.

Different cultures. Still, that was how the situation was at that moment. Nevertheless, my mediating Italian attitude pushed me, after some time, to ask the executive chef: 'Hey, what about if he cleans the dishes?' as I was also watching the time passing and thinking of the up coming meals to be served with 50 percent of my work force missing.

Akira looked at me horrified, of course conscious that the penalty of being kicked out of the kitchen was surely not enough for the 'high crime' of inefficency, and still missing a good suicide commitment. I don't know if he was right, but Masa, finally, went to wash dishes and we managed to serve dinner that night. They didn't work for long together.

Still, I learned my first lesson that day, of professional efficency and how a kitchen has to be properly directed. I remember so many times in which we worked in a kitchen with fewer staff than the previous day, but managed to do so much more and so much better. Better one person in a kitchen who loves his job, than three who are there just to make some money. And discipline is the only rule for doing this work for more than the mentioned two years. Discipline and kitchen organization.

A. M.

"Wake up! Wake up! It's three o'clock!" Agnes shook her roommate awake. It was three o'clock! "What are you talking about?" Ursula replied groggily.

"It's three o'clock! Let's go!" Agnes's green eyes were wide in panic. Her roommate checked her watch and saw that it was, in fact, three o'clock in the afternoon.

"So what? It's three o'clock. What's wrong with you?" Agnes blinked, slowly realizing there was no significance to "three o'clock." Siesta had begun at two and the Montali staff was not expected to return to work for another hour. In her sleepy haze, she had awoken with a start and, after looking at her clock, believed that three o'clock was late for something.

To the young men and women of the Country House Montali staff, work is everything. All in their early to mid-twenties, they travel from different parts of the world, sever themselves from the lives they have grown comfortable in, and work anywhere from 14 to 17 hours a day, six days a week, for seven months. This, in combination with being 15 minutes away from the nearest town by car, results in being completely consumed by the hotel and restaurant life. For many, the amount of work or the distance from home is too much and they leave. For the rest, it is a personal commitment that they are determined to make the most of. There is an innate fear in each of them of being late. Even if, like Agnes, they are not.

The opportunity to live and work in Italy is a dream that many do not have the time or reason to pursue. To a young chef, the chance to immerse oneself in the study of Italian cuisine, in a real Italian kitchen, is amazing. They know there will be hardships and ordeals, as there are in any workplace, but any shortcomings or inconveniences are quickly overshadowed because, Guess what? I'm going to Italy, baby! No matter how much one emotionally gears up for any difficulties, no one can be fully prepared for the baptism-by-fire that is the first month.

Depending on the individual, the adjustment period is challenging for a number of reasons. The idea of living in the Italian countryside may be a bucolic fantasy to some. For a city person, learning to cohabit with insects and strange mountain creatures, can become a shocking and inescapable reality.

Later on you learn that when you live in a wood, you will more frequently come across wild boar while driving at night and pheasant during the day, than cars on the road. You just have to get used to it.

The Country House Montali is packed with peculiarities. It is a gourmet vegetarian restaurant in the heart of Italy with a Brazilian head chef. The food is prepared and served by Slovakians, Mexicans, Asians, Poles, Swedes and Americans. In such a diverse staff, miscommunication is bound to occur regularly. At times it can cause needless drama, and at others can serve as much needed comic relief in a tense situation.

One evening, the restaurant was packed with people and the last of the primi had been served. The stress level had been mounting in the kitchen since the afternoon and the extreme heat only added to everyone's irritability. Janko turned to Marta and said, "Marta, isn't it you washed pans?" At Marta's confused look, Marketa intervened and said, "Marta, have you already washed the pans?" After Marta nodded, Marketa turned to Janko and joked in her accented English, "Janko, you really must work on your grammar." "What are you talking about? My grandma is 87 years old!" Janko responded, sending everyone rolling on the floor.

To many, the workload is the easiest aspect of Montali life to adjust to. By the third or fourth month, a comfortable routine is in place. The chefs begin seeing the rotation of dishes come back around, familiarizing themselves with Malu's cooking style, and the waiting staff have a clear idea of their daily responsibilities in addition to serving dinner at night. However, while speed and efficiency improve noticeably, there is also the visible wear and tear of nerves. As one member of the team put it, "You can feel so lonely in a huge city like Los Angeles with millions of people surrounding you, but claustrophobic at the top of a mountain with only eight other people." Inevitably, people lose it.

Nobody knows better than Malu and Alberto that working at Montali is difficult. To them, their restaurant and hotel is their life, a choice and passion. If every member of their staff puts as much love into their work as they did, life could not be better. On their part, Malu and Alberto make an effort to make sure every one of their employees feels as settled or comfortable as possible.

In the same light, there is a common thread among those who stay and work for the entire season. Not only do they possess an incredible work ethic, they feel committed to both the restaurant and the decisions that they have made. Malu and Alberto see these individuals as gold. They are people who come in everyday leaving all of their worries behind and work as if Montali is their own.

Sustaining this level of work, this level of professionalism, is not without reward. Many of the young men and women who come do so to learn about themselves, the kinds of people they want to become and the limits that they can excel beyond. It is a sabbatical for those in their mid-twenties and a chance to study a unique cuisine with various people from all over the world. In return for imparting such an enormous amount of time, chefs feel real ownership of their efforts, contributions and creativity. They learn to delegate their time and maximize physical efficiency, to clear the mind and only focus on the task at hand. It is an incredible period of self-discovery and growth.

Towards the end of the season, the weather cools down significantly and staff members slowly trickle home one by one. The warmth of the kitchen compared to the chilly weather creates a cosy environment and Malu, Alberto and the Montali staff enjoy everyone's company more than ever. The end of the season looms closely, meaning the 'family' will soon be dispersed around the globe.

When the staff passes through the front gates, they don't know if they will ever see the hotel, Malu, Alberto or each other again. They leave with both a sense of pride for having fulfilled their commitment, and a devotion to the people they have come to love.

They dwell on how far they have come as individuals rather than how much catching up there is to do in their lives back home. They will remember learning how to drive the manual old Fiat Uno with over 160,000 miles on the clock, passing the shepherd and his grazing sheep every morning, and the suicidal bunny that chose the exact moment they drove by to race across the road. They realize they've become accustomed to the insects in their bathtub, the spiders in their sink, and the leg cramps that recurrently shocked them awake at three in the morning. They remember small traditions they've created for each other, the unparalleled view of Lake Trasimeno from their medieval castle's apartment window, and the countless 'a la salutes' at Happy Hour.

Nobody knows if they will ever become good chefs, but surely in Montali they have built foundations for it.

160

THE VEGETERRANEAN

APPRENTICE

In our long restaurateurs' life, we have worked with a lot of different chefs. Chefs can be very difficult people: temperamental, moody, primadonna types, and they have always been quite complicated characters to work with.

Luckily the executive chef in the hotel is my own wife, so we can depend much less on others. Still we have always needed some good help for a relatively complicated cuisine. We often found that young chefs who had already got cookery school training, and were also willing to do some professional apprentice work, were in general the best guys to use. They are the ones ready to put in a real effort and research to master the profession. Relatively young, they were also a bit easier to handle

than older chefs, and they were generally very motivated to learn new skills. And I personally love motivation.

There are no cookery schools that give specific courses on vegetarian cuisine even though there is a greater demand for low fat and good tasting diets, making our courses even more interesting from a professional point of view. The idea also that our unique cuisine could spread a little more around the world through these happy young people was, and still is, a source of special satisfaction for us. I still remember the very excited e-mail from one of our previous chefs, happily writing how the band 'Black Sabbath' had gone to a restaurant where he was working in

Kansas and asked for 12 vegetarian meals. The terrified owner, who didn't have any special recipes for veggies nor knew that Matthew had been trained at Montali, was scared to death by the appalling looking group and ran to the kitchen seeking any help from his chef.

Great was the general satisfaction when our previous cook announced he had no problems with that specific request, but even greater when Black Sabbath loved the food and went back for dinner on three consecutive days.

This is a pleasure to us as well, sharing Matthew's pride in showing a widely developed culinary skill to his boss and to his good looking clients as well. But of course it isn't always like that. Life may be more of a struggle than pleasure and people reflect life – life that is not easy in Montali. We run a seasonal business and everybody used to this work knows how hard it is to make your annual income while officially being open to the public only half the year. You literally have to do one year's work in half that time. The working hours are so hard, starting at eight in the morning and ending at midnight sometimes. This makes the days long and not everyone is capable of working so many hours. The hotel life looks more like a type of retreat where you are expected to run most of the time and keep going. "Take no prisoners."

It is generally more a question of rhythm and working attitude because otherwise my wife and I would already be dead. Many people simply don't manage. But the ones who do will gain a fantastic experience and will be able to work in the future under any circumstances and conditions, with no problem of time or hardship. This is quite common for any successful restaurant or hotel nowadays. They will be the tough ones who have made it. The others will run away through the season.

That is how a seasonal tourist job is. Lots of fun because you are located in a paradise but lots of work as well. A bit like working on a cruise! It is quite hard to make a choice when, at the beginning of the season, we collect resumes of the new applicants. How do you choose a chef from a small jpeg picture and a one page CV which may not mean anything? I remember one chef sending a great picture of himself in an impeccable white chef's uniform and a gold medal, looking like Jean Paul Bocuse. Wow! How impressive! But then it was a surprise to discover later on that he had been a drug addict for many years, ended up in jail four times and was living on antidepressant pills to keep going!! Wow! Not a person who would manage 15 hours a day. He did in fact only work two weeks and then, there I was, without one chef in the middle of the season.

Researchers have also proven that 70 percent of CVs are false or exaggerated. A guy wrote to me once claiming he had been working for Celine Dion at her personal house. I found out later he had just worked as a waiter in a chain of Canadian fast foods that seemed to be owned by the famous singer.

Another had been 'head-of-garcons' in the Hilton in Prague …pity he was there only carrying suitcases as a porter! That's how recruitment goes sometimes, you must follow your feelings, making a choice and hoping it was a good one producing a good person. In all cases, the seven months' long season will surely be full of those 'special' moments in which the lady workers will burst into tears and the gents will start smoking from their noses as a consequence of work.

It is impossible to make any rules. Sometimes men are easier to handle than women because they are less emotive. Sometimes it is just the other way around because women can be milder. Sometimes Americans can be easier than British, sometimes not. We had one Korean male chef who was boring and stubborn. We have a Korean female chef who is writing this book with me, and she is the embodiment of energy, cleverness and good humour. It is so difficult to make a choice at recruitment time.

Running a seasonal business makes it more complicated as we have to restart and train most of the staff every year, which is such an endless job and sometimes tiring. Mostly, it depends on the person you end up dealing with. It is such a nice thing when you find someone willing to learn and ready to dedicate their energy to the job. It is such a pain when you have someone who doesn't give a dime and isn't willing to learn. The big problem is that youngsters having to work as waiters think: "I'm not a servant." That's a very common current mentality for a whole generation, diminishing a job that anybody should be proud of instead! Aren't we all servants anyway? Everybody in life serves someone else. But pride has gone, unfortunately, for the majority.

It is such a great pleasure instead to see a slow chef ending his season 'running' in the kitchen, or watching how a bakery chef has learned desserts and starters, or seeing a 'not so sophisticated' waitress ending the season behaving finally like a lady. Those are some of the satisfactions in our work, at least to balance the times in which you really get mad.

I remember one time in which, after a lovely dinner, I was enjoying the company of some of my guests while sipping some wine on the outer veranda. A girl from the staff came to ask the gentlemen if they would like another drink.

After that she also kindly asked me if I wanted one. I ordered a glass of Grecale, a chilled sweet after-dinner wine which I am pretty fond of. The attractive young girl went to get the drinks and some of my clients commented on how my life could seem like a dream to many. The pergola where we were sitting was covered with fully blossoming jasmine and honeysuckle flowers and the wonderful aroma spread through the romantic night on that isolated hill. Montali is a gorgeous spot and the views of the valley were breathtaking on that full moon night. One of the gentleman said to me: "Hey Alberto, you really live like a king here." He said this exactly when the young girl, just having returned with the drinks, (very elegantly) stumbled across the veranda giving me the sweetest bath of all my life. Of course, the life of King Alberto didn't last long and people had a glimpse of how animated a hotelier's life can be.

Naturally, as a boss you always know that often you are just simply hated by many of your employees, regardless of how much fun they can be having. Montali for instance can be a lot of fun: the staff spending nights drinking different drinks on the house, afternoon siesta hours sunbathing by the pool, every day eating top gourmet food, sightseeing with the hotel car in all the fabulous medieval towns in Umbria and beyond. Tough life! But all this gets forgotten when the boss shouts. He is just a jerk of course, even if such a place would not exist without a jerk keeping it going. Still, in the long run I know my staff loves me, even when I shout, and everybody admits that some shouting makes work progress much better.

A.M.

Secondi

SECOND COURSES

SPIEDINI PRIMAVERA

Spring vegetable skewers. An intriguing succession of grilled vegetables and seitan on a skewer. This colourful dish is great for a buffet.

Serves 6   Ⓜ   *95 minutes*

INGREDIENTS

1 aubergine, thinly sliced lengthwise

3 tablespoons chopped parsley, plus 1 whole sprig

4 garlic cloves, thinly sliced

2 courgettes, thinly sliced lengthwise

1 red bell pepper

1 tablespoon celery leaves

1 orange

6 small endives, halved lengthwise

3½ carrots, peeled

1 teaspoon white wine vinegar

1 shallot, finely chopped

1½ tablespoons chopped celery

½ quantity Seitan, cut into 2.5 cm (1") squares (see page 35)

1 tablespoon flour

2 tablespoons white wine

2 slices pineapple

Salt and pepper to taste

Extra virgin olive oil

———

Aubergine: Grill and transfer to a bowl. Drizzle with oil and season with salt, pepper, 1 tablespoon of the chopped parsley and a fifth of the sliced garlic. Set aside.

Courgettes: Follow the same procedure as the aubergine.

Pepper: Blacken and peel the bell pepper (see page 20), cut into 2.5 cm (1") squares, and fold in the celery leaves, a fifth of the sliced garlic, a little oil and salt

Orange: Use a serrated knife to peel off the rind and skin of the orange, leaving the pulp exposed. Slice into 1 cm (½") pieces and quarter into wedges.

Endives: Grill the halves and season with oil, salt and pepper.

Carrots: Cut three into pieces 1 cm (½") wide. Steam until al dente, transfer to a bowl and season with salt, pepper, the remaining chopped parsley, a fifth of the sliced garlic, olive oil and 1 teaspoon white wine vinegar.

Seitan: Sauté the shallot, remaining garlic, celery and the remaining ½ carrot in 4 tablespoons extra virgin olive oil for 2 minutes. Add the seitan and parsley sprig and cook over a high heat until the seitan begins to brown. Sprinkle with the flour and cook for 1 minute. Add the wine and cook until evaporated. Taste for seasoning.

Pineapple: Peel, core and slice into 2.5 cm (1") wide rounds. Cut each slice into eight wedges.

TOPPING

3 tablespoons breadcrumbs

½ tablespoon chopped parsley

½ tablespoon chopped basil

1 small garlic clove, puréed

1 teaspoon extra virgin olive oil

Salt to taste

———

Combine all the ingredients together in a bowl.

ASSEMBLY

On 12 skewers, arrange one piece of each component in this order: courgette, aubergine, endive, carrot, pepper, seitan, orange, courgette, aubergine, onion, carrot, pepper, seitan and pineapple. Arrange the skewers on a tray, sprinkle with topping and bake at Gas Mark 4/180°C/350°F for 10 minutes. Serve hot.

QUICHE di PORRI

A buttery-crusted leek quiche, fit for a dinner party or a Sunday brunch.

Serves 8 Ⓜ *45 minutes & 30 minutes chilling & 20 minutes baking*

DOUGH

250 g (9 oz) Italian '00' flour
Pinch of salt
125 g (4½ oz) butter, melted and slightly cooled to room temperature
1 egg, lightly beaten
3 tablespoons of water, if needed

———

Combine the flour and salt on a flat surface and make a well in the centre. Add the butter and egg into the well and gently work with your fingertips until a dough begins to form. Incorporate by cutting through the dough with a pastry cutter and rolling back together, three or four times, until the texture and colour is even, adding water if too dry. Wrap in plastic film and refrigerate for 30 minutes.

FILLING

500 g (1 lb 2 oz) leeks, white and yellow parts only
600 ml (20 fl oz) milk
165 ml (5½ fl oz) single cream
Salt to taste

———

Clean the leeks well. Thinly slice on a mandolin and combine the rounds with the milk in a large sauté pan. Cook over a low heat until the consistency is creamy, like that of a beaten egg. Coarsely blend, keeping some large pieces. Mix in the cream and season with salt. Cool to room temperature.

ASSEMBLY

Roll the dough between two sheets of floured parchment paper into a round disc 33 cm (13") in diameter. Remove the top layer of parchment paper and place eight 7 cm (3") pie tins face-down over the dough. With a small knife, cut round discs 1 cm (½") around the rims of the tins. Invert and gently press the dough into the bottom, edges and sides. Pierce the bases with a fork a few times and spread some of the leek mixture over each base. Run the teeth of a fork evenly over the surface of each tart in concentric circles. Bake in an oven at Gas Mark 4/180°C/350°F oven for 20 minutes. Serve hot.

RULLO di SPINACI e RICOTTA

Spinach and ricotta cheese roulade. An Italian classic where spinach accompanies ricotta in a soft creamy dream. All enveloped by a crunchy light pastry.

Serves 4 **D** *45 minutes & 30 minutes baking*

FILLING

150 g (5½ oz) spinach, cooked and squeezed
½ tablespoon butter
Salt and black pepper to taste

150 g (5½ oz) fresh ricotta, drained
of excess liquid
30 g (1 oz) grated Parmesan
1 pinch of nutmeg

———

Finely chop the spinach and sauté in a medium-sized pan with the butter. Season to taste and cool completely. In a medium-sized bowl, work the ricotta with a fork until creamy. Mix the Parmesan and nutmeg into the ricotta. Fold in the cooled spinach and mix. Season to taste, cover and set aside.

DOUGH

125 g (4½ oz) Italian '00' flour, plus more for dusting
1 pinch of salt
60 g (2 oz) butter, softened and cut into chunks

1 egg, lightly beaten
½ teaspoon water

———

Sift the flour and salt into a bowl and make a well in the centre. Add the butter to the well and work into the flour with your fingertips until the dough resembles a coarse meal. Scoop handfuls of dough into your hands and gently rub between your palms. Repeat until the dough reaches a sand-like consistency and all ithe ngredients are well incorporated. Add the egg and, using a pinching motion, work into the dough until a ball begins to form. Knead for 1 minute until smooth. Pick up the dough and forcefully throw it down onto the work surface 20 times. Cover with plastic film and refrigerate for 15 minutes. Roll out the dough on a floured surface into an 28 x 33 cm (11 x 13") rectangle, short side facing you. Loosely roll dough around a rolling pin, then unroll on a large sheet of parchment paper. Use a pizza cutter to even the edges.

ASSEMBLY

2 tablespoons single cream, mixed with 1 tablespoon of milk, for brushing

———

Preheat the oven to Gas Mark 4/180°C/350°F. Mix the single cream and milk in a small cup and brush the entire surface of the dough with cream. Spread the filling over the surface, leaving a 2.5 cm (1") border across the top uncovered. Gently roll in the sides. Using the paper as a guide, start from the bottom and roll upwards, creating a log shape. Brush the surface with more cream. Transfer, using the paper as the base, to a baking sheet and bake for 30 minutes. Cool for a few minutes before slicing and serving.

This dish can be prepared and baked 1 day in advance. Reheat at Gas Mark 2/150°C/300°F for 10 minutes, then increase the temperature to Gas Mark 4/180°C/350°F and bake for an additional 5 minutes.

COXINHAS ENCANTADAS

An incomparable version of the Brazilian tear-drop shaped fried pastry, stuffed with a creamy aubergine filling. As lovely as it is delicious, this dish is a definite crowd-pleaser.

Serves 6 Ⓜ *55 minutes*

FILLING

1 small garlic clove, minced

1 teaspoon thyme leaves

1 tablespoon chopped onion

2 tablespoons extra virgin olive oil

1 aubergine, peeled and cubed

Salt and pepper to taste

1 tablespoon grated Parmesan

1 tablespoon grated Pecorino Romano

———

Sauté the garlic, thyme and onion in olive oil for 1 minute. Add the aubergine and season with salt and pepper. Cook until the aubergine is soft and dry, about 20 minutes. Purée in a blender and cool completely before mixing in the cheeses.

DOUGH

1 small potato

120 ml (4 fl oz) Vegetable Stock (see page 36)

120 ml (4 fl oz) milk

1 tablespoon butter

½ teaspoon salt

125 g (4¼ oz) flour

———

Cook, peel and mash the potato and set it aside. In a saucepan bring the stock, milk, butter and salt to a boil. Add the flour all at once and stir immediately. Continue to stir for 5 minutes or until the dough begins to dry and pull away from the bottom of the pot. Remove from the heat and mix with the potato. On a flat surface, knead the dough for 2 minutes.

ASSEMBLY

2 tablespoons flour

60 g (2 oz) breadcrumbs

2 whole eggs, beaten and lightly salted

Vegetable oil, for deep frying

Salt to taste

———

Roll 1 round tablespoon of dough into a ball and flatten into a 6 cm (2½") disc. Place 1 teaspoon of aubergine mixture in the centre and close the dough around it, taking care not to break the dough. Seal gently and mould into a pear shape. Repeat with the remaining dough.

Place the flour, breadcrumbs and eggs in separate bowls. One by one, neatly coat each coxinha with first flour, then egg and lastly breadcrumbs. Set aside on a plate. Heat the vegetable oil and fry in batches to a golden brown. Transfer to a tray lined with paper towels and season with salt. Serve hot.

PASTICCIO di MELANZANE

An aubergine tart, served with a Caper Parsley Sauce. A great dish for any special occasion. The tart blends with the salty caper sauce in a fusion of pure pleasure. A favourite of many of our clients.

Serves 8   (M)   *30 minutes & 25 minutes baking*

PASTICCIO

3 aubergines, peeled and cubed into 5 mm (¼") pieces

200 g (7 oz) Scamorza cheese, cubed into 5 mm (¼") pieces

2 eggs, lightly beaten

40 g (1½ oz) grated Parmesan

2 garlic cloves, mashed

1 tablespoon oregano

Salt and pepper to taste

———

Soak the cubed aubergines in cool water for 10 minutes. Drain, squeeze and place in a large pot over a high heat. Cook the aubergine by itself, stirring occasionally, until softened and nearly dry. Cool to room temperature. Fold in the Scamorza, eggs, grated Parmesan, garlic and oregano and mix well. Season with salt and black pepper. Line the bottom of a 23 cm (9") spring-form tin with parchment paper and grease lightly. Spoon the mixture into the tin and, using a fork, spread evenly. Set aside.

CAPER PARSLEY SAUCE

1 tablespoon capers

2 tablespoons parsley

Extra virgin olive oil to cover

———

Wash and rinse the capers. Chop with the parsley, then combine with olive oil in a small bowl. Set aside.

TO SERVE

Half an hour before serving, bake the pasticcio at Gas Mark 4/180°C/350°F for 25 minutes. Remove from the tin and cut into wedges. Serve immediately, topping with 1 tablespoon of Caper Parsley Sauce.

Enhance this dish further with servings of Carrot Purée (see page 212), Beetroot Salad (see page 213) and a drizzle of Pepper Sauce (see page 31).

SFORMATINI di ZUCCHINE

A soft, creamy ricotta cheese and courgette flan with a hint of marjoram. A dish of true refinement with the addition of a Parmesan cheese shell.

Serves 6 (M) *25 minutes & 20 minutes baking*

INGREDIENTS

2 tablespoons extra virgin olive oil

1 shallot, finely chopped

2 courgettes, coarsely grated

1 teaspoon dry marjoram

White pepper and salt to taste

100 g (3½ oz) ricotta

1 tablespoon grated Parmesan

1 egg

2 egg whites

———

Heat the oil and shallot together in a pan for 30 seconds then add the courgettes, marjoram and white pepper. Cook until the courgettes are soft and dry, tossing occasionally (approximately 15 minutes). Remove from the heat and cool. In a bowl, work the ricotta and Parmesan with a fork until very creamy. Beat the egg yolk and whites together, and mix into the ricotta until the mixture is smooth. Combine with the cooked courgettes and season to taste.

Preheat the oven to Gas Mark 4/180° C/350°F. Bring a medium pot of water to a boil. Butter six individual miniature muffin tins (or a muffin pan), preferably silicon. Line the bottom with small squares of parchment paper. Divide the mixture evenly among the tins and place in a baking dish. Carefully pour hot water into the baking dish until it reaches halfway up the sides of the tins. Cover with aluminium foil and bake for 20 minutes.

PARMESAN SHELL

Butter

12 tablespoons grated Parmesan cheese

———

Melt the butter in a non-stick pan over a medium-high heat. Sprinkle 2 tablespoons of grated Parmesan into a 13 cm (5") round shape. When the cheese is melted, use a spatula and carefully transfer the cheese wafers from the pan to an inverted and greased ramekin. Press gently with your fingers to give it a shell-like shape. Cool for 1 minute, then transfer, flat-side down, onto a sheet of parchment paper. Repeat with the remaining cheese.

TO SERVE

One quantity Truffle Sauce (see page 36)

———

Transfer the Parmesan shells to individual plates, place a flan inside each one and garnish with Truffle Sauce to serve.

If Truffle Sauce is not available, use Olive Sauce (see page 30).

INVOLTINI di MELANZANE

Aubergine spring rolls. A delightful Mediterranean taste with cherry tomatoes contrasting with the fried aubergine. Lovely with a filling of buffalo mozzarella.

Serves 6 Ⓜ *35 minutes & 15 minutes baking*

AUBERGINE

4 medium aubergines, peeled and sliced lengthwise into 5 mm (¼") pieces

420 g (15 oz) Italian '00' flour

Sunflower oil, for frying

Salt to taste

3 mozzarella balls

24 basil leaves

———

Submerge the aubergines in water with 1 tablespoon flour for 15 minutes. Meanwhile, heat the oil. Drain the aubergines from the water, pressing two slices at a time between your palms, and arrange over a colander to dry. Cover the slices with flour to coat all sides. Fry in the hot oil until golden-brown and transfer to a tray lined with paper towels. Cool for 2 minutes, then gently press each slice between clean paper towels to get rid of any excess oil. Season with salt. Slice the mozzarella into rounds 6 mm (⅓") thick, and cut again into 6 mm (⅓") wide strips. Place one piece of mozzarella and one basil leaf across the lower third of each aubergine slice and gently roll up (makes 24 rolls).

ASSEMBLY

18 cherry tomatoes, quartered

3 garlic cloves, sliced thinly

Extra virgin olive oil

Salt and pepper to taste

5 basil leaves, coarsely chopped

———

Toss the tomatoes with the garlic, oil, salt, pepper and basil and drizzle with more olive oil until well-combined. Layer half the seasoned tomatoes over the bottom of a 20 × 20 cm (8 x 8") baking dish. Line the aubergine rolls on top and top with the remaining tomatoes. Bake at Gas Mark 4/180°C/350°, uncovered, for 15 minutes and serve hot.

RULLO di SCAROLA

Escarole roulade. The slightly bitter taste of this endive fuses perfectly with the fresh Crescenza cheese. The texture of the pine nuts and breadcrumbs makes each bite of this dish a symphony of delight.

Serves 8 Ⓜ *20 minutes & 15 minutes proofing & 35 minutes baking*

INGREDIENTS

3 tablespoons extra virgin olive oil

3 garlic cloves, 2 whole and 1 puréed

40 g (1½ oz) black olives, pitted and chopped

4 heads escarole, roughly chopped

35 g (1¼ oz) pine nuts, lightly toasted

85 g (3 oz) re-hydrated raisins

Salt to taste

4 tablespoons breadcrumbs

1 tablespoon butter

1½ tablespoons chopped mixed herbs
    (basil, sage, chives)

Single cream for brushing

4 tablespoons Crescenza or soft creamy
    cheese

———

Sauté the whole garlic cloves and black olives in the olive oil until coloured. Add the escarole and toss to cook until any liquid is evaporated. Season with salt and fold in the pine nuts and raisins. Toast the breadcrumbs in the butter until golden brown. Transfer to a bowl and mix in the herbs and puréed garlic. Set aside.

DOUGH

250 g (9 oz) Italian '00' flour

125 ml (4 fl oz) water

3 tablespoons butter, at room temperature

Pinch of salt

———

Sift the flour on to a flat surface. Make a well in the centre, add the water, butter and salt and work with your fingers until a dough begins to form. Knead for 30 seconds, then forcefully throw the dough on to the work surface 100 times. Cover with a warm glass bowl for 15 minutes (the glass bowl can be heated for 1 minute in a warm oven). Flour a clean cloth. Shape the dough into a disc and slowly roll over your wrists to open. When the dough begins to thin (but not break), place on the cloth and gently pull into a rectangular shape, maintaining thickness, approximately 46 x 25 cm (18 x 10"). The dough should be slightly transparent. Trim the edges with a pizza cutter.

ASSEMBLY

Brush cream over the dough surface and sprinkle with the breadcrumb mixture. Dot the filling and cheese evenly over the crumbs, leaving a 1 cm (½") margin on top uncovered. Use the cloth as a guide and fold in the sides. Pull the cloth up from the bottom corners and gently roll up the roulade. At the top, continue to roll on to a sheet of parchment paper until the seam side is down. Brush the surface with more cream. Transfer, with the parchment paper, on to a baking sheet. Bake at Gas Mark 4/180°C/350°F for 35 minutes or until golden. Slice and serve warm.

SFORMATINO MEDITERRANEO

A dish made to impress all the senses. This courgette and ricotta cheese mélange is served over a Beetroot Sauce and garnished with fried carrots.

Serves 6 (M) *45 minutes & 25 minutes baking*

OUTSIDE

3 courgettes, sliced thinly and grilled

1 garlic clove, sliced

1 tablespoon chopped parsley

Salt and pepper to taste

2 tablespoons extra virgin olive oil

———

Marinate the grilled courgettes with the remaining ingredients and set aside for half an hour.

FILLING

240 g (8½ oz) ricotta

2 tablespoons grated Parmesan

40 g (1½ oz) Pecorino di Pienza, cut into small cubes

1 egg, lightly beaten

Salt and pepper to taste

———

Beat the ricotta with a fork until very creamy. Add the remaining ingredients, mix well and set aside.

BEETROOT SAUCE

1 medium beetroot, steamed and puréed

2 tablespoons Vegetable Stock (see page 36)

3 tablespoons plain yoghurt

1 tablespoon parsley, chopped

1 teaspoon lemon juice

1 tablespoon extra virgin olive oil

Salt and white pepper to taste

———

Pass the beetroot purée through a sieve and mix well with remaining ingredients.

FRIED CARROTS

3 carrots, peeled and shaved with a vegetable peeler

Vegetable oil, for deep frying

———

Deep fry the carrot shavings in hot oil until crispy. Drain over paper towels and season with salt.

ASSEMBLY

Line the bottom of six muffin cups or ramekins with cut-out squares of parchment paper. Line with slices of courgette, allowing them to overhang. Spoon the filling into the cups and close the courgettes over the top. Place in a roasting pan with 5 cm (2") sides and fill with boiling water halfway up the sides of the cups. Cover with a sheet of parchment paper and bake at Gas Mark 4/180°C/350° for 25 minutes. Remove the cups from the water and carefully invert each one with the aid of a wide spatula. Coat the bottom of each serving plate with a ladle of warm Beetroot Sauce. Gently place the courgette mélanges in the centre of the sauce and top with the fried carrots. Serve immediately.

PARMIGIANA alla CASERTANA

A variation of Parmigiana di Melanzane. A classic southern Italian dish from the town of Caserta, this is a favourite, especially among vegan guests.

Serves 6 Ⓜ *50 minutes*

INGREDIENTS

700 g (1½ lb) aubergines, peeled and sliced into 5 mm (¼") rounds

Italian '00' Flour, for coating

Vegetable oil

3 medium onions, peeled and sliced thinly on a mandolin

2 tablespoons extra virgin olive oil

2 tablespoons capers, rinsed and drained if packed in brine, and chopped

2 tablespoons black olives, pitted and chopped

2 tablespoons green olives, pitted and chopped

1 tablespoon pine nuts, toasted

2 tablespoons raisins, rehydrated

5 tomatoes, peeled, deseeded and roughly chopped

5 basil leaves, roughly chopped

1 tablespoon red wine vinegar

Salt and pepper to taste

———

Soak the aubergine in water mixed with 1 tablespoon of flour for 15 minutes. Drain off the water and press each round between your palms to squeeze out any excess water. Coat each piece in flour and place on a large tray. Deep fry the aubergines in vegetable oil until golden brown. Transfer to a tray lined with paper towels and pat with more paper towels to soak up the excess oil (aubergines will naturally absorb a lot of oil). Cool.

Meanwhile, in a large pan, cook the onion rounds in 2 tablespoons of olive oil. Caramelise slowly over a low heat, stirring occasionally, for 30 minutes or until golden-brown and dry. Mix in the ingredients from the capers to basil and cook for an additional minute before adding the vinegar. Season with salt and pepper and cook for one more minute or until the vinegar has evaporated.

ASSEMBLY

Spread a third of the onion mixture over the bottom of a 23 x 33 cm (9 x 13") casserole dish. Overlap half the aubergines over the onion mixture and sprinkle with salt. Add another third of the onion mixture, layer the remaining aubergines on top and sprinkle with salt. Top with the final third of onions and press the surface gently with the back of the spoon. Bake at Gas Mark 4/180°C/350°F, uncovered, for 5 minutes. Cut serving portions with clean scissors and serve hot.

CANNOLI di RADICCHIO e PERE

Radicchio, pear and smoked cheese rolls. A very sophisticated recipe, with a unique blend of tastes. It's surprising how the sweetness of the pear matches the bitterness of the radicchio and works with the smoked cheese. A winning taste.

Serves 4 (M) *35 minutes & 20 minutes baking*

FILLING

1 radicchio, cut into eight wedges (held together at the core)

2 tablespoons extra virgin olive oil, plus more for drizzling

Salt and pepper to taste

1 pear, peeled and cored

2 garlic cloves

1 shallot, finely chopped

1 tablespoon chopped walnuts

2 tablespoons white wine

2 teaspoons red wine vinegar

———

Drizzle the radicchio eighths with olive oil and season with salt and pepper. Grill all sides on a grill pan and cool before chopping coarsely. Slice the pear into 5 mm (¼") pieces and grill in the same manner. Cool briefly before cutting into 5 mm (¼") cubes and tossing with the radicchio. Sauté the garlic and shallot in olive oil until the garlic is coloured and the shallot is transparent. Discard the garlic and add the radicchio and pear. Cook for an additional 2 minutes, then add the walnuts, wine and vinegar. Cook until the liquid has evaporated, about 10 minutes. Season with salt and pepper and drain over a colander. Cool completely.

ASSEMBLY

250 g (8½ oz) Puff Pastry (see page 32)

28 g (1 oz) Taleggio, cut into 1 cm (½") cubes

28 g (1 oz) smoked Scamorza, cut into (½") cubes

1 egg yolk, for brushing

———

Roll out the puff pastry over a flat surface into a large rectangle 2 mm (⅛) thick. With a pizza cutter or sharp knife, cut it into 9 cm (3½") squares. Spread 2 tablespoons of filling over one side of each square, leaving a 5 mm (¼") border around the edges, and top the filling with the cheeses. Brush the borders with egg yolk. Loosely roll the uncovered side over the filling to create a cylinder-shape and gently press the edges to seal. Brush the entire surface with egg yolk. Bake at Gas Mark 4/180°C/350°F for 20 minutes. Serve hot.

THE VEGETERRANEAN SECONDI

PARMIGIANA di ZUCCHINE

Courgette parmigiana. A twist on the classic version. Traditionally made with aubergines, this recipe calls for courgettes. The light crispy batter that surrounds the vegetables melts with the béchamel and tomato sauce in a delicious way. A real Italian treat.

Serves 6 (M) *60 minutes*

INGREDIENTS

90 g (3½ oz) flour

90 g (3½ oz) cornflour

Salt to taste

210 ml (7 fl oz) beer

Vegetable oil, for deep frying

4 courgettes, sliced thinly lengthwise on a mandolin

375 ml (12 fl oz) Tomato Sauce (see page 36)

1 quantity Basic Béchamel (see page 26)

42 g (1½ oz) grated Parmesan

60 g (2 oz) Pecorino di Pienza, cubed

85 g (3 oz) mozzarella, cubed

In a bowl, combine the flour, cornflour, a pinch of salt and beer and whisk until smooth. Heat the vegetable oil in a large deep-fryer. When the oil is hot, dip the courgettes into the batter and deep-fry in batches until golden brown and crispy. Remove with a slotted spoon and set on paper towels to drain, seasoning with a sprinkle of salt. Set aside to cool.

ASSEMBLY

Drizzle a third of the Tomato Sauce over the bottom of a 20 x 20 cm (8 x 12") baking pan or oven-proof casserole dish and add drops of Basic Béchamel. Layer the courgettes side by side. Sprinkle with half the grated Parmesan and cubed Pecorino di Pienza. Pour over another third of the Tomato Sauce and Basic Béchamel and repeat the layering process, finally topping with mozzarella. Bake at Gas Mark 4/180°C/350° for 20 minutes, or until golden brown and bubbly. Remove from the heat and serve hot.

GATEAU di PATATE

Individual potato delights with the distinct earthy flavour of smoked Provolone cheese.

Serves 6 (M) *15 minutes & 30 minutes baking*

INGREDIENTS

3 large potatoes

40 g (1½) oz butter

2 eggs, lightly beaten

2 tablespoons extra virgin olive oil

2 tablespoons grated Parmesan

1 tablespoon grated Pecorino Romano

Salt, black pepper and white pepper to taste

Olive oil for greasing

Breadcrumbs

28 g (1 oz) smoked Provolone cheese, cut into small cubes

_____

Cook and peel the potatoes. Mash well with the butter in a bowl and cool. When at room temperature, mix in the remaining ingredients minus the oil, smoked cheese and breadcrumbs. Grease six 5 cm (2") ramekins and dust with breadcrumbs. Layer the bottoms with a small piece of parchment paper.

ASSEMBLY

Divide half the mixture among the ramekins. Layer with the smoked cheese cubes and top with the remaining mixture. Use the teeth of a fork to draw concentric circles over the top. Top with dots of butter, bake at Gas Mark 4/180°C/350 °F for 30 minutes and serve hot.

If smoked Provolone is not available, use a different mild smoked cheese.

PIZZA e MINESTRA

Of humble origins, a crunchy corn flour 'pizza' is combined with wild dandelion greens and minestra (vegetable broth) for a hearty soup. This dish comes from the region of Molise in central Italy and is enjoyed by both poor and rich alike.

Serves 8   E   *25 minutes & 30 minutes baking*

BAKED POLENTA

4 tablespoons extra virgin olive oil, plus more for drizzling

2 tablespoons breadcrumbs

250 g (9 oz) fine polenta

140 ml (5 fl oz) water

140 ml (5 fl oz) milk

1 teaspoon salt

―――――

Line the bottom of a non-stick 28 cm (11") spring-form baking tin with parchment paper. Drizzle a generous amount of olive oil over the bottom and sprinkle the breadcrumbs over the oil. Toast the polenta in a dry sauté pan over medium heat until barely coloured and transfer to a bowl. Mix in 2 tablespoons of olive oil and the remaining ingredients and pour into the prepared pan. Press gently to spread out and create indentations all over the surface with your fingertips. Drizzle more oil over the top and bake at Gas Mark 3/170°C/340°F for 30 minutes or until golden brown and crunchy on top. Remove from the heat, cool for a few minutes until manageable and invert onto a flat surface. Cut into 1 cm (½") cubes and set aside.

DANDELION GREENS

900 g (2 lb) dandelion greens

4 garlic cloves

1 small cayenne pepper, sliced

60 ml (2 fl oz) extra virgin olive oil

Salt to taste

240 ml (8 fl oz) Vegetable Stock (see page 36)

―――――

Bring a pot of lightly salted water to a boil and cook the greens for a few seconds. Transfer to a plate. Sauté the garlic and pepper in olive oil until brown. Add the dandelion greens and sauté for an additional minute, seasoning to taste with salt. Add the polenta cubes and vegetable stock and continue to cook for 3 minutes. Taste for seasoning and serve hot.

STRUDEL di ZUCCHINE

The rich addition of roasted pine nuts and basil leaves gives this courgette and Taleggio strudel a very special touch. Enjoy for a formal dinner or a nice casual lunch.

Serves 8 Ⓓ *45 minutes & cooling time & 35 minutes baking*

FILLING

2 garlic cloves

3 tablespoons extra virgin olive oil

1 tablespoon pine nuts

4 courgettes, grated

Salt and white pepper to taste

180 g (6½ oz) ricotta

2 tablespoons grated Parmesan

Pinch of nutmeg

_____

Sauté the garlic cloves in olive oil until they begin to brown. Toss in the pine nuts and toast. Add the grated courgettes and cook until all the water released has evaporated and the courgettes begin to colour. Season with salt and white pepper and remove the garlic cloves. Set aside and cool completely. In another bowl mix the ricotta, Parmesan and nutmeg together and then add it to the cold courgette. Set aside.

DOUGH

100 g (3½ oz) Italian '00' flour

100 g (3½ oz) Grano Duro flour

2 tablespoons extra virgin olive oil

1 egg white

90 ml (3 fl oz) water

Pinch of salt

_____

Sift both flours on to a dry, flat surface. Make a well in the centre and add the remaining dough ingredients. Work with your fingers to incorporate until a dough forms. Gather the dough and knead until the consistency is even throughout. Throw the ball of dough down on to the work surface 50 times, then cover with a warm glass bowl for 15 minutes (the glass bowl can be heated for 1 minute in a warm oven).

ASSEMBLY

2 tablespoons single cream mixed with 1 tablespoon milk, for brushing

80 g (3 oz) Taleggio, roughly cut

4 fresh basil leaves, coarsely chopped

_____

Place a clean cloth on a dry surface and flour. When the dough has rested, shape into a disc and slowly roll over your wrists to open. When it begins to thin (but not break), place on the cloth and gently pull the dough into a rectangular shape with your fingers, maintaining thickness. The dough should be thin and slightly transparent. Trim the edges with a pizza cutter. Brush the surface with the cream and milk mixture.

Dot the courgette filling evenly over the dough, leaving a 2 cm (¾") margin on top uncovered. Repeat with the ricotta mixture and the Taleggio and sprinkle with basil. Use the cloth as a guide and gently fold in the sides of the pastry. Pull up the cloth from the bottom corners and gently roll up the strudel to the top until the seam side is down. Place on a baking tray lined with parchment paper, brush the surface with cream and milk, then bake for 35 minutes at Gas Mark 4/180°C/350°F or until golden brown. Cool for a few minutes before slicing and serving.

MELANZANE RIPIENE

Stuffed aubergine. A succulent traditional dish. Thyme and marjoram enhance the great taste of the ingredients. It's even better if cooked in a terracotta casserole dish. You will see the difference.

Serves 4   Ⓜ   *25 minutes & 1 hour cooking*

INGREDIENTS

5 medium-sized long aubergines

Sea salt

1 medium shallot, finely chopped

1 garlic clove, chopped

1 teaspoon marjoram

1 teaspoon thyme leaves

45 ml (1½ fl oz) extra virgin olive oil

Salt, black pepper and white pepper to taste

1 tablespoon chopped parsley

90 g (3 oz) crustless bread slices, soaked in milk

1 tablespoon grated Parmesan

1 tablespoon grated Pecorino Romano

1 tablespoon grated Fossa cheese

8 basil leaves

140 g (5 oz) mozzarella, sliced into 8 pieces

———

Wash the aubergines and trim the ends. Cut four aubergines into 6 cm (2½") long pieces. Using a melon-baller, scoop out the inside of the aubergine, leaving 5 mm (¼") of flesh around the rim. Reserve the scooped out portion. Lightly sprinkle sea salt on the inside of the cylinders and place, upright, in a colander for 10 minutes. Rinse off the excess salt and place the aubergines upside down on a towel or cloth to dry. Peel the fifth aubergine and chop with the reserved flesh.

Sauté the shallot, garlic, marjoram and thyme in olive oil for 1 minute, then add the chopped aubergine. Season with a pinch of salt and black pepper and continue to cook for 20 minutes more, stirring occasionally. Cook until the aubergine mixture is soft and excess water has evaporated. Remove from the heat and add the chopped parsley. Cool completely. Squeeze any excess milk from the bread and add the bread to the mixture. Add the grated cheeses and mix.

SAUCE

450 g (1 lb) cherry tomatoes, halved

2 medium garlic cloves, sliced

4 basil leaves, roughly chopped

60 ml (2 fl oz) extra virgin olive oil

Salt and black pepper to taste

———

Mix all the sauce ingredients in a bowl and season to taste.

ASSEMBLY

Layer the sauce in a heavy-bottomed 25 cm (10") casserole dish with a 7 mm (3") rim. Fill each cylinder with the aubergine filling and insert a basil leaf. Place each piece, upright, over the tomatoes in the pan. Cover the casserole dish with parchment paper and a lid. Cook over a low heat for 1 hour. Turn off the heat and place one slice of mozzarella over each piece. Serve hot, with sauce.

POLPETTONE di SEITAN VESTITO

'Polpettone' translates to meat loaf. In the Montali version, meat is substituted with seitan and encased in puff pastry. Delicious with Tartar Sauce.

Serves 4 **D** *65 minutes*

SEITAN FILLING

1 small shallot, finely chopped

1 small garlic clove, minced

½ carrot, sliced crosswise

½ stick celery, sliced crosswise

1 bunch parsley, plus 1 tablespoon chopped

1 tablespoon butter

2 tablespoons extra virgin olive oil

350 g (12 oz) Seitan, cut into 1 cm (½")
  cubes (see page 35)

55 g (2 oz) ricotta

½ tablespoon flour

2 tablespoons white wine

Salt, pepper and nutmeg to taste

Zest of ½ lemon

2 tablespoons grated Parmesan

1 tablespoon grated Pecorino Romano

1 egg plus 1 yolk

28 g (1 oz) bread cubes, crustless, soaked
  in milk for 3 minutes, then squeezed to drain

———

Sauté the vegetables and parsley, but excluding the chopped parsley, in butter and oil for 30 seconds. Add the seitan, cook for 2 minutes, then sprinkle with flour and continue to cook. Add the wine to break down the flour and cook until the liquid has evaporated. Cool completely. Remove the parsley and purée the seitan in a blender. Mix in the chopped parsley, nutmeg, salt, pepper, lemon zest, cheeses, egg and breadcrumbs. Set aside.

PUMPKIN

60 g (2 oz) pumpkin flesh

———

Carefully peel the pumpkin and keep the piece as whole as possible. Steam until al dente. Remove from the heat and cool. Cut into long sticks so that the ends are 1 cm (½") squares.

ASSEMBLY

225 g (8 oz) Puff Pastry (see page 32)

1 egg yolk, for brushing

1 tablespoon sesame seeds

———

Soak a 33 x 33 cm (13 x 13") sheet of parchment paper in water. Gently ring out the excess liquid and lay out on a flat surface. Spread the seitan mixture into a 23 x 23 cm (9 x 9") square on the paper, aligned with the bottom centre of the sheet. Line the pumpkin 20 cm (8") across horizontally, 5 cm (2") from the bottom. Lift the bottom of the paper and tightly roll the seitan around the pumpkin into a long log shape. Close the ends of the paper like a candy wrapper and place inside a 23 x 13 cm (9 x 5") loaf tin. Bake at Gas Mark 4/180°C/350°F for 40 minutes. Remove and cool completely.

Open the puff pastry to an 28 x 23 cm (11 x 9") rectangle. Brush the edges with egg yolk. Unwrap the seitan from the paper and place towards the bottom of the pastry.

Roll gently, as before. Brush the whole surface with egg yolk and sprinkle with sesame seeds. Bake again at Gas Mark 4/180°C/350°F for 20 minutes. Cool for a few minutes before slicing and serving.

PORRI al MONTASIO

The delicate sweetness of leeks combines well with the sour taste of Montasio cheese. This is great to eat with fried puffy bread discs.

Serves 4   E   *20 minutes & 70 minutes resting*

INGREDIENTS

675 g (1½ lb) leeks, white and yellow parts only
2 tablespoons butter
2½ tablespoons flour
500 ml (16 fl oz) milk
Salt, pepper and nutmeg to taste
150 g (5 oz) Montasio or Cheddar cheese, cut into 1 cm (½") cubes

———

Clean the leeks and cut each into three equal pieces. Halve each cylinder crosswise on a bias. Cook in lightly salted boiling water for 3 minutes and set aside. In a separate saucepan, melt the butter and add the flour. Stir until the roux is golden brown and add a quarter of the milk, stirring simultaneously until smooth. Add the remaining milk and cook until thickened, approximately 3 minutes. Stir two-thirds of the cheese into the sauce until melted. Season with salt, pepper and nutmeg.

ASSEMBLY

Butter the bottom of a 20 x 20 cm (8 x 8") ceramic plate. Stand the leeks bias-side up and drizzle with the sauce. Top with the remaining cheese and bake at Gas Mark 4/180°C/350°F for 10 minutes or until the cheese is bubbly and golden brown. Serve hot with Bread Discs.

BREAD DISCS

140 g (5 oz) Italian '00' flour, plus more for dusting
1 teaspoon fresh yeast
170 ml (5½ fl oz) warm water
2 teaspoons extra virgin olive oil
¼ teaspoon salt
Vegetable oil for frying

———

Sift the flour into a large bowl and make a well in the centre. In a separate bowl, mix the remaining ingredients together then pour into the well. Work the dough in a wave-like motion to incorporate air. When the colour and texture are smooth, cover with plastic film and rest in a warm, dry place for 35 minutes. Then sprinkle the surface of the dough with flour and 'turn' it by pulling small portions of the dough around the edge towards the opposite side of the bowl. Once one full turn has been made, repeat twice, starting by sprinkling more flour. Rest for 35 more minutes.

Dust a flat surface with flour and roll the dough into a flat 2 mm (⅛") thick disc. Cut out rounds with a 6 cm (2¼") round cutter. Deep fry in vegetable oil, drain over paper towels, and season with salt. Serve hot.

TORTINO di SCAROLA e PORRI

Escarole and leek tart. The crunchy pastry and the just sautéed vegetables make a pleasant and light sweet and sour taste. Wonderful at a buffet party.

Serves 5 (M) *60 minutes & cooling time*

DOUGH

168 g (6½ oz) Italian '00' flour, plus more for dusting
1¼ teaspoon salt
84 g (3 oz) butter, at room temperature and cut into small cubes
1½ tablespoons cold water

_____

Combine the flour and salt in a medium-sized bowl. Work in the butter with your fingertips until the mixture becomes crumbly. Collect handfuls of dough and gently rub between your palms. Continue this movement to achieve a sand-like texture. Add the water and continue to work with your fingertips until the dough comes together. Gather into a ball and wrap in plastic film. Refrigerate for 30 minutes.

Roll out the dough between two sheets of parchment paper dusted with flour, creating a large rectangle approximately 43 x 28 cm (17 x 11"), and 3 mm (⅛") thick. Butter six individual 9 cm (3½") pie tins with butter. Use a small knife to cut the dough into discs slightly bigger than the tins. Gently use the dough to line the tins. Pierce the dough bases with a fork and bake at Gas Mark 4/180°C/350°F for 10 minutes. Remove from the heat and cool completely before gently removing the pastry from the tin.

FILLING

35 g (1¼ oz) pitted black olives, roughly chopped
2 large garlic cloves, peeled
5 tablespoons extra virgin olive oil
1 escarole, roughly chopped
Salt and pepper to taste
2 tablespoons raisins, rehydrated with port wine and drained
1 whole leek, white and yellow parts only, julienned
70 g (2½ oz) soft sheep's cheese, cut into 5 mm (¼") cubes

_____

Sauté the olives with 1 garlic clove in half the olive oil. Cook for 30 seconds before adding the escarole. Season with salt and black pepper and cook slowly over a medium heat for 20 minutes, half covered. Add the raisins and cook uncovered for 2 minutes. Remove the garlic. In a separate sauté pan, cook the leeks with the remaining garlic and olive oil over a medium heat until tender, approximately 10 minutes. Remove the garlic and fold the leeks into the escarole mixture.

ASSEMBLY

Divide half the cubed cheese between the six pie crusts and spread evenly over the bottom of each. Divide the filling and cover the cheese. Top the filling with the remaining cheese and set aside until ready to serve. Reheat on a sheet tray for 5 minutes at Gas Mark 4/180°C/350°F or until the cheese is melted and bubbly. Serve immediately.

FAGOTTINI di PASTA SFOGLIA FARCITE con COUSCOUS

Puff pastry envelopes filled with a spiced couscous. An Italian touch added to a north African dish with an Asian hint!

Serves 8   Ⓜ   *45 minutes*

COUSCOUS

45 g (1½ oz) peas

1 small garlic clove

14 g (½ oz) butter

1½ tablespoons olive oil, plus more for drizzling

1 teaspoon ground cumin

1 teaspoon curry powder

1 tablespoon ginger, peeled and grated

½ celery stalk, chopped

1 small carrot, cut into 5 mm (¼") pieces

½ courgette, cut into 5 mm (¼") pieces

42 g (1½ oz) cauliflower, broken into small florets

1 small shallot, finely chopped

Salt and pepper to taste

42 g (1½ oz) couscous

42 ml (1½ fl oz) Vegetable Stock (see page 36)

1½ tablespoons pine nuts, lightly toasted

2 tablespoons raisins, soaked in hot water
  and drained

In a small pot, combine the peas with enough water to barely cover them, salt and a drizzle of extra virgin olive oil. Cook over a medium heat until the peas are just cooked, approximately 10 minutes. Drain the water and set aside. Sauté the garlic in the butter and olive oil in a large pan. When the garlic browns, add the cumin, curry powder and ginger. Toss in the remaining vegetables and cook to al dente, seasoning with salt and pepper. Toast the couscous in a non-stick pan to golden-brown and set aside in a bowl. Bring the stock up to a boil and immediately pour on to the couscous. Cover and leave for 10 minutes. Uncover, flake with a fork and add to the vegetables. Fold in the pine nuts, drained raisins and peas. Cool completely.

PUFF PASTRY

500 g (17½ oz) Puff Pastry (see page 32)

1 egg, beaten, for brushing

ASSEMBLY

30 g (1 oz) Pecorino di Pienza, cut into flat 2.5 cm (1") squares

Roll out the puff pastry into a large rectangle, approximately 3 mm (⅛") thick. Using a pizza cutter, cut the pastry into 12 cm (4½") squares. Fill with 2 tablespoons of the couscous mixture and one square of cheese. Fold over two diagonally opposite corners of each square, sealing one over the other with egg wash. Brush the other two corners with egg wash, fold over and press gently to seal. Brush the surfaces with more egg wash and set the parcels on a baking sheet lined with parchment paper. Bake at Gas Mark 4/180°C/350°F for 20 minutes. Serve hot.

EMPADINHAS

This Brazilian savoury pastry of African origin is traditionally filled with various meats, but the Montali version features delectable palm hearts and green olives.

Serves 6 Ⓜ *60 minutes*

FILLING

1 shallot, chopped

1 tablespoon extra virgin olive oil

60 g (2 oz) green olives, pitted and chopped, plus 6 olives left whole

1 tablespoon fresh parsley, chopped

180 g (6½ oz) palm hearts, chopped

6 tablespoons water

½ quantity Basic Béchamel (see page 26)

Salt and pepper to taste

———

Sauté the shallot in the oil until translucent. Add the chopped olives, half the parsley, palm hearts and water and cook, covered, for 5 minutes. Stir in the Basic Béchamel and cook for an additional minute. Mix in the remaining parsley, season to taste and remove from the heat. Cool completely.

DOUGH

150 g (4 oz) flour

½ teaspoon salt

90 g (3 oz) butter, cut into cubes
   and softened

1 egg

———

In a medium bowl, combine the flour, salt and butter and work with your fingertips until the dough resembles coarse crumbs. Gather a handful and gently brush your palms together, allowing the dough to fall back into the bowl. Continue until it reaches a sand-like consistency. Add the eggs, incorporating into the dough. With the help of a pastry cutter, continually cut through the dough and work well with your hands until it is even in colour and texture. Wrap in plastic film and refrigerate for 15 minutes.

ASSEMBLY

1 egg, beaten, for brushing

———

Using two sheets of parchment paper that have been dusted with flour roll out two-thirds of the dough (leaving the rest wrapped) into a large disc that is 5 mm (¼") thick. Using a 12 cm (4½") round cutter, cut out six discs. Evenly line six ramekins with the dough so that it comes three-quarters of the way up the sides. Fill each with 1 tablespoon of filling. Placee one whole olive in the centre and top with one more tablespoon of filling. Roll out the remaining dough in the same matter as before but slightly thinner. Using a round cutter slightly smaller than the rim of the ramekin, cut six equal discs. Gently press over the filling. Seal the sides to the top with a small knife, working around the edge of the ramekin to create a nice frame. With the remaining dough, roll six 5 mm (¼") balls to be used to top the pastry lids. Brush the surfaces with the egg and bake at Gas Mark 4/180°C/350°F for 20 minutes. Serve hot.

"We're staying at a what?" Gene asked incredulously as his brother, Joe, pulled in through the entrance gates.

"A vegetarian restaurant and hotel," Joe repeated.

"Oh. That's what I thought you said." Gene and Rob exchanged surprised glances. The month-long trip to Italy was a long time coming and their brother, Joe, the designated itinerary planner, had decided to tell them this now. They laughed at the irony.

The DiSimone brothers from Boston, Massachusetts, were in Umbria for the largest steak festival in the world. La Sagra della Bistecca is held every August in Cortona, and for years the brothers had heard tales of the streets of the medieval city lined with impossibly long grills and smouldering cuts of tender meat brilliantly ablaze at every turn. In 2002, the three devoted meat lovers were looking forward to the festival as one of the major highlights of their trip.

As they pulled up in front of the Country House Montali, none of them knew what to expect. Whether it was the beautiful pictures he had seen online, the convenient distance from Cortona or plain curiosity about a vegetarian restaurant and hotel, Joe had booked himself and his brothers in for two nights. He, like Gene and Rob, had a preconceived notion of the hotel based on the term 'vegetarian'. In Boston, vegetarianism was not so much an eating preference as a campaign to save the world.

Which is what they thought Montali might be like until they saw Alberto chain-smoking Marlboro Reds outside his office. He greeted them warmly, showed them to their room and informed them that dinner would be at eight in the evening. Joe, Gene and Rob nodded politely and settled in. They didn't anticipate eating much at dinner, which did not bother them as they planned to head straight to the festival immediately afterwards anyway.

Later, they sat down at dinner, admired the beautiful setting of the dining room and discussed the peaceful ambience, but their thoughts were already three hours ahead. However, with each course that Alberto brought and introduced to their table, they grew more and more amazed. The food was incredible.

The completely satiated brothers ended up going to the festival, much to the bemusement of Alberto, but their meal there was not nearly as memorable as the one they had just had. Or the one they had the following night. By the time the three brothers left Montali, they had fallen in love with the food, the surroundings, the quiet, the opportunity to get to know other guests and the whole relaxing experience. Their emotions had been strained since the passing of their mother nine months earlier, and, after quarrelling through the first half of their trip, they were filled with a tremendous sense of calm, which they had not had together in a long time.

The following year, Joe came back to Montali with his brothers and his girlfriend, Sara Concannon. They had met while working on a case together a few years before, he as a sergeant detective for the Boston police and she as an assistant district attorney. Like Joe and his brothers, she was completely charmed by Montali. She loved that there was no menu at all and that dinner was a surprise every night, impeccably presented and delectably prepared. She was introduced to a whole variety of dishes that, out of unfamiliarity, she might have passed over at other restaurants.

Over the next few years, Joe and Sara continued to come back to Montali. They spent late nights talking with Alberto outside on the veranda, quickly developed favourite dishes (which Malu took note of) and became very comfortable and familiar with the property, its surroundings and each other.

October 23, 2004, was a day that all three brothers remember well for different reasons. After lengthy culinary studies in Italy, chef Rob returned to Boston. On another side of town, Gene was beside himself that evening when the Red Sox won game one of the World Series. And in a quiet restaurant, Joe celebrated his birthday by asking Sara to spend every birthday for the rest of their lives together. It was a good day for everyone.

Neither Joe nor Sara cared for a swanky wedding at the Yacht Club or a ritzy hotel in Boston. They decided very early on that they wanted a small wedding with family and intimate friends in a setting that would be special to both of them. Moreover, Joe had close friends and family in Europe. Montali could provide a warm and personal setting, delicious food and, particularly, an opportunity to share with those closest to them this treasure of a hotel that they had been raving about.

As dear as Joe and Sara had become, Malu and Alberto took it upon themselves to take care of

everything. From the menu to the paperwork to the entertainment and all the minute details in between, everything was taken care of. Alberto ordered flower arrangements, travelled back and forth to Perugia for stacks upon stacks of papers and set up hair appointments at the best salon in the local town for the morning of the wedding. The salon was not even open on Mondays, the day of the wedding, but Alberto had somehow convinced them to not only open, but also to do so at 7:30 in the morning, two and a half hours before normal opening hours on any other day.

The five-night, five-day holiday for Sara, Joe and their wedding guests was full of relaxation, succulent foods and elegant musical entertainment. Filling the restaurant, they chatted and sipped wine late into the evening and spent the days travelling or lounging by the pool. For the staff, it was five 17 hour working days, running like mad and functioning on a mixture of caffeine and pure adrenaline. The chefs tried to prepare as many things in advance as they could, but the nature and intricacies of most of the courses demanded that the dishes be prepared fresh and on the day they were served.

Regardless of how intensely anyone worked, Malu worked ten times harder. Somewhere between Sunday night and Monday morning, she had prepared hundreds of assorted delicate Brazilian confections, miniature quiche cups, dozens upon dozens of ricotta-stuffed cannelloni, various sauces and the wedding cake. When the chefs groggily rolled into the restaurant on Monday morning they looked at Malu in wonder and amazement as she vigorously smacked a rug against a brick wall while calling out to them, "Ciao, Ragazzi!" The bright eyes and fresh glow of the skin fooled no one; everyone knew that she had barely slept.

The guests began to refer to Alberto as Mr. Rourke from the hit 1970s show Fantasy Island, as he made sure everything flowed perfectly. Before they even knew they were warm, Alberto had already opened a window. When indecisive about which wine they wanted to drink, Alberto brought out the perfect selection. Whatever need they might have, Alberto anticipated it.

On the day of the wedding, the guests left early to attend a ceremony in a local church. When they returned, they had barely stepped out of the cars before Alberto, Agnes and Marketa were standing before them with celebratory champagne flutes of chilled Bellini. A harpist and flautist performed under the veranda and the guests lounged under the shade, enjoying the miniature pizzas and pies that were being passed around. Inside the kitchen, Daniel was in the middle of pouring Cachaça into a punch bowl filled with a fruit juice cocktail when Malu walked by and dipped a cup into the bowl to taste.

"Daniel, it needs something more... It needs more tequila!" She said after taking a sip.

"Malu, there's already a whole bottle and a half in there," Daniel replied.

Malu's eyes opened wide and she said, "Basta!" She turned her attention to the miniature Pecorino Romano and walnut breads that had just come out of the oven. "Okay, slice them in half, spread red pepper pâté over them and give them to the girls to pass around" she instructed, before once more redirecting her attention to the cannelloni in the oven.

Joe, Sara and the guests had no idea what was on the menu for the day and, assuming that the hors d'oeuvres were the 'light lunch', happily devoured them. When the primo of ricotta cheese-stuffed cannelloni and saffron risotto arrived on individual plates, they were pleasantly surprised. Once those plates were replaced by the secondi of coxinhas and puff pastry-encased olives and palm hearts, they were stuffed. By the time the Brazilian confections, silky-smooth chocolates dipped in chocolate sprinkles or coconut shavings, were passed around, guests were in 'nirvana'.

A rest and a few more drinks and finally people were ready for the last touch: the wedding cake.

From the kitchen the four usually invisible chefs came out, beautifully and cleanly dressed carrying the highlight of their working week – a double-layered carrot cake with a layer of apricot marmalade in the middle, covered in chocolate ganache and decorated with a fresh peony and double cream. All the guests greeted them with thanks and joy.

Joe and Sara presented Alberto and Malu with gifts of their appreciation. For Malu, a classy black designer tote bag and, for Alberto, a bottle of Mondavi & Rothschild Opus One, a Californian special. Later, Alberto walked into the kitchen and faced the staff that he knew he had been driving to the ground for days. He saw their bloodshot eyes and bandage-covered fingers. "I know I haven't said this yet, but I wanted to tell you how proud I am of all the work you have done over the last few days. Really proud." And with that, he instructed Marketa to open the bottle of Opus One and distribute it among the staff. He smiled to himself as they clinked their glasses in an 'a la salute!' toast before walking outside to the back to enjoy it amongst themselves for a few precious minutes.

How the wedding party managed to eat dinner only a few short hours after the reception is a mystery. Yet they all showed up and enjoyed every course from the Crudite di Pere e Melone antipasti to the Vulcano di Cioccolato dessert, all while a cello and violin were performing in the dining room. After dinner, they sat outside facing the stone stage that Alberto had illuminated with a single lamp. Two opera singers performed classical Italian pieces like 'O Sole Mio' and 'Time to Say Goodbye' with the accompaniment of a pianist. The tenor, standing proudly with a colourful scarf wrapped around his neck, captivated the crowd with his deep resonating voice. In a shimmering black dress billowing in the breeze of the late summer night, the soprano

sang in a brilliant, crystal-clear tone that carried across the grove. Malu had pulled out chairs for the staff and insisted that they each grab a glass of wine and enjoy the concert outside, an order that they were all happy to obey.

The wedding celebration was, for both the party and the staff, an event to remember. On several late nights the staff would gather around the marble table after everyone had left, cleaning stemware with silk cloths to a spotless shine. Blasting loud dance music past midnight, they would keep their eyes forced open and bob up and down to the beat of the music to stay awake. They would go home, nurse their chapped hands and completely collapse, only to wake a few hours later to start all over. There were tears of exhaustion, shouting matches and periods of comatose silence. There were those who needed lively conversation to stay alert, and others who resorted to robot-like behaviour as a means to carry on.

More importantly, Joe and Sara's guests were able to experience the beloved Montali they had heard countless stories about for so many years. Above all, they met the legendary Alberto with his tales and adventures from all over the world and Malu, his beautiful Brazilian wife and culinary wonder.

Best of all, there were no stressful details to worry over. Joe and Sara simply showed up and enjoyed themselves. As it had since the first time the DiSimone brothers came in 2002, Montali provided them with exactly what they were looking for before they even knew it themselves.

Assortito

SIDES

Broad Bean Purée
Serves 6

60 g (2 oz) dried broad beans, rinsed

½ carrot, halved lengthwise

2 garlic cloves

½ medium onion, quartered

1 sprig parsley

2 tablespoons extra virgin olive oil

Salt to taste

350 ml (11½ fl oz) water

1 tablespoon lemon juice

1 tablespoon tahini

———

Combine the beans, carrot, 1 whole garlic clove, onion, parsley, 1 tablespoon olive oil, salt and water in a large pot and cook over a low heat for 40 minutes, or until the beans are tender. Remove the beans and purée them in a blender. Discard the other used ingredients. Purée the remaining garlic clove and add to the beans, along with the lemon juice, tahini and remaining olive oil. Season to taste. Cover and set aside.

Carrot Purée
Serves 6

5 carrots, peeled

1 tablespoon butter

1 shallot, finely chopped

Salt and black pepper to taste

2 tablespoons grated Parmesan

½ tablespoon parsley, finely chopped

½ tablespoon chives, finely chopped

———

Cut the carrots into 5 cm (2") pieces that are equal in size and steam until al dente. Sauté in the butter with the chopped shallot and season with salt and pepper. Purée in a blender and set aside. When cooled completely, fold in the grated cheese, parsley and chives. Taste for seasoning, adding more salt and pepper if desired. Serve at room temperature.

Fried Courgette Flowers
Serves 6

7 tablespoons flour

5 tablespoons cornflour

3 pinches salt

140 ml (6 fl oz) beer

60 g (2 oz) Pecorino di Pienza

12 courgette flowers

Vegetable oil, for frying

———

Mix the flour, cornflour, salt and beer together to make a batter. Cut the cheese into 12 narrow sticks. Remove the centres from the courgette flowers and replace them with a stick of cheese. Dip in the batter and deep fry in oil. Transfer from the oil to a pan lined with paper towels and season with salt. Serve immediately.

Corn and Apple Salad
Serves 6

½ head sweetcorn, steamed

1 Granny Smith apple

1 shallot, finely chopped

1 tablespoon chopped parsley

3 tablespoons extra virgin olive oil

Red wine vinegar to taste

Balsamic vinegar to taste

Lemon juice to taste

Salt and pepper to taste

1 dash Tabasco

——————

Cut the corn kernels from the ears. Peel, core and cube the apple to the same size as the corn kernels. Toss all ingredients together. Allow to sit for at least 2 hours before serving to allow all the flavours to combine.

Beetroot Salad
Serves 8

300 g (10 oz) beetroot, parboiled

100 g (3½ oz) yoghurt

2 tablespoons grated Feta

Salt and black pepper to taste

1 tablespoon creamy goat's cheese

2 teaspoons parsley, finely chopped

2 tablespoons extra virgin olive oil

Lemon juice to taste

——————

Coarsely grate the beetroot and fold in the remaining ingredients. Taste for seasoning. Serve chilled or at room temperature.

Aubergine 'alla Siciliana'
Serves 6

Vegetable oil, for deep frying

1 large aubergine

Salt and pepper to taste

1 medium celery stalk, coarsely chopped

1 tablespoon extra virgin olive oil

1 tablespoon butter

1 ripe tomato, peeled and deseeded

1 tablespoon pine nuts, toasted

1 tablespoon raisins, rinsed

4 basil leaves

½ tablespoon sugar

3 teaspoons red wine vinegar

——————

Heat the oil in a large, heavy-bottomed pot. Peel the skin from the aubergine in 2.5 cm (1") strips so that the aubergine looks striped. Cut into 2.5 cm (1") cubes and fry in the hot oil until browned. Remove with a slotted spoon and drain on paper towels. Season with salt and black pepper and cool to room temperature. Meanwhile, sauté the celery in oil and butter over a medium heat until translucent. Add the chopped tomato and cook until most of the liquid released from the tomato has evaporated. Stir in the aubergine, pine nuts, raisins and basil leaves, torn with your fingers. Sprinkle with the sugar and vinegar and continue to cook for 3 minutes. Remove from the heat and cool. Allow to rest for 1 hour to blend the flavours. Reheat before serving.

The relentless heat of late June seeped through the stone walls of the small kitchen where Malu and three chefs were working. A large pot of water was boiling on the six-top, creating a sauna-like effect and adding to the moisture in the air that clung to everyone's skin. Earlier, there had been a lovely breeze running through the kitchen from outside but, after it had repeatedly extinguished the flames on the gas stove, it had had to be shut out.

Grace stopped grilling slices of courgette long enough to aerate her long-sleeved chef's jacket and fan her neck. Janko, also melting in the heat, turned to her and asked, "Grace, are you happy?" As if on cue, Grace faced him with a solemn expression and replied, "Yes. Yes, I am happy. But I could be happier." This was their special code for, 'Oh, you know what time it is.' Without a word, Janko stepped out of the kitchen and returned with four glasses of chilled house white wine with single cubes of ice floating on top. Passing them around, the chefs stood around the large marble table where they were all working raised their glasses for a quick 'a la salute' and clinked glasses. The crisp wine was a welcome relief from the sweltering heat and Daniel, another chef from the USA, pressed the cold glass to his forehead before setting it down. Instantaneously, all the chefs returned to work.

With a four-course menu that changes daily, there are two things that remain constant from one day to the next: soft and airy ciabatta served hot and fresh from the oven for the guests and Happy Hour for the kitchen and waiting staff. As the ciabatta should begin baking by 7.30 pm to ensure a timely service, Happy Hour must commence by seven o'clock at the very latest. Both are taken very seriously, and absolutely no evening would be complete without them.

A young waiter from California did not know how seriously Happy Hour was taken until he made the mistake of asking Malu, when requested by her to pour wine, if he could use plastic cups instead of wine glasses to avoid washing extra dishes. Without a moment's hesitation, Malu said, "This is our one pleasure! We have to do it the right way. We can't enjoy wine out of a plastic cup!" (It should be noted here that when the Montali staff drink margaritas, the fruits are freshly squeezed and served in salt-rimmed glasses with a lemon wedge twist.)

Happy Hour of the Montali variety was started by Malu to serve two purposes. The first and most obvious was to provide a daily source of enjoyment for both back and front of house staff. Every employee works at least 12 hours a day for six days a week, and looking forward to Happy Hour makes each working day that much more agreeable. The second purpose was a clever ploy to ensure that everyone works to his or her maximum capability. There are few other environments as stressful and overwrought with tension as a restaurant kitchen. Starting from the hour before dinner service until the second the last aperitif is served, nervous energies collide among chefs and waiters. A relaxed restaurant staff is both unrealistic and undesireable. The constant sense of urgency pushes individuals to work harder, faster, creating a dynamic, adrenaline-pumping atmosphere that chefs thrive off. On the other hand, an over-anxious person is likely to slip up and make a nervous blunder. Enter Happy Hour, serving to ever so slightly ease the tension before the big push.

One evening earlier in the season, Malu looked up from the lasagne dough that she was diligently kneading on the wooden board and squinted at the clock. "Is it time?" she asked to no one in particular. One of the other chefs laughed, understanding her question perfectly, and Malu called to one of the Slovakian waitresses, "Hey, man! It's time to make Happy Hour!" The waitress grinned and left the room to get the wine glasses from behind the bar. When she came back into the kitchen half a minute later, she was awkwardly holding five glasses in her hands, fingers and stems clumsily intertwined. She tried setting the glasses down on the large marble table where the chefs were working and, unsurprisingly, toppled one glass over another. Shards scattered like dust across the surface of the marble into plates, bowls and trays holding food that had taken hours to prepare for the evening's dinner.

In any other restaurant kitchen, this kind of mistake would warrant absolute rage and fury from any chef. Meticulously picking through food was out of the question, and everything in the danger zone had to be thrown away. As a result, the chefs would have to work three times as fast for the remainder of the evening to make up for the discarded food.

Malu, clearly distressed, placed her fingertips at her temples and, after a moment, said to the waitress, "Don't make me paranoid, baby! From now on, glass cannot be placed on the table or near the food. It's too dangerous! Please don't stress me." If she was infuriated, she did not let it show. She spoke to the girl in an even, completely non-threatening tone, like a mother reprimanding her child.

Working quickly, she began reorganizing the pre-dinner preparation time while the other two chefs, keeping their mouths shut, silently swept away the mess. They sadly resigned themselves to the fact that Happy Hour was cancelled, until Malu stood straight, put her hands on her hips and said to the waitress, "At least pour us some wine, baby, or else we can't relax." A few minutes later, the girl returned and distributed wine to the chefs. When she handed Malu her glass, tears sprang to her eyes and she lowered her gaze. Malu lightly pinched her cheek and gave her a quick hug.

In the summertime, cool house white wine is a common choice as it's light and plentiful from the large jug in the wine fridge. Malu and Alberto also store half-cases of Rapitala solely for the staff to drink when one prefers a nice red wine, or when one of the waiting staff needs practice opening bottles.

Malu also sees Happy Hour as a time to taste new vintages that are introduced in the local markets and insists that the chefs taste them as well. One can hardly argue with her when she says, "Our chefs must know the good wines!" The beauty of Happy Hour is that it is in no way limited by the quality of the beverage. (Quantity, on the other hand, is at one's own discretion and rarely, if ever, abused.) When Daniel arrived from California, the first thing he did was prepare an ice-cold sour lemon margarita for each person. The very next day, he saw a pile of leftover chopped fruit and immediately put together a pitcher of sangria.

On her day off, Grace wanted nothing more than to eat watermelon all day and drove 20 minutes down the mountain to MaxiSidis, the largest market in the local town. After finishing only half of what she bought, she took the rest into work the next day and kept it chilled in the fridge.

Janko had told her about a slushy watermelon tequila cocktail and she was determined to try it out. At five in the evening, she cut the watermelon into pieces, being careful to reserve all the juice, deseeded it and puréed it in a blender before pushing it through a sieve. Marketa and Agnes helped her with the cocktail, adding not only tequila but also a splash of cranberry liquor and the juice of two lemons. Janko tasted the juice, nodded in approval and placed it on a rimmed metal tray to freeze quickly.

By seven o'clock, Janko and Grace removed the bowl from the freezer. It was very cold, but still completely liquid. Grace turned to Janko and said, "It's ice cold. Shall I pour?" "No. The liquid has to have at least a film of ice. Put it back in the freezer. We'll drink it when it's ready." Grace smiled and obeyed. She turned to Marketa and said, "Quality Control. I like his style."

Tu proverai si come sa di sale

Lo pane altrui e com' è duro calle

Lo scendere e il salir per l'altrui scale

~DANTE, PARADISO, 17, 58.60

"Thou shalt prove how salty tastes another's bread, and how hard a path it is to go up and down another's stairs." As a Florentine in exile, Dante speaks of the sadness of adapting to the food far from home, and the difficulties of finding work. While saltless bread may taste flavourless to many, the plainness had been adapted by the palates of the Florentine and Umbrian long before Dante's time and has remained so to the present day.

Pane, Focacce & Pizza
BREADS

The absence of salt in Tuscan bread making began in the twelfth century during the vigorous development of Pisa and Florence. Conflict ensued between the two cities and Pisa blocked salt commerce to Florence, who was forced to import salt from elsewhere at a significantly higher cost. Hundreds of years later, Pope Paul III heavily increased the already high salt tax, affecting Perugia, Umbria, Lazio, Marche and Romagna. All areas relied heavily on salt for the flavouring and preservation of foods but, in an effort to fight the overbearing system, boycotted the use of salt in breads. Even after the 'Salt War' ended, Tuscan and Umbrian bakers continued to bake their breads without salt.

PANINI

Not to be confused with popular pressed sandwiches, these miniature breads are a favourite among the Montali guests and staff. While these are a few examples of the freshly-baked breads that we serve daily, feel free to improvise with other ingredients to create your own panino.

12 breads Ⓔ *15 minutes & 115 minutes rising & 13 minutes baking*

WALNUT AND PECORINO ROMANO PANINO

230 g (8 oz) Manitoba flour
45 g (1½ oz) grated Pecorino Romano
45 g (1½ oz) walnuts, chopped
Black pepper to taste

160 ml (5½ fl oz) warm water
1 teaspoon salt
3 g (⅛ oz) fresh yeast

PIZZA PANINO

230 g (8 oz) Manitoba flour
1 tablespoon dried oregano
4 sundried tomatoes, coarsely chopped
70 g (2½ oz) black olives, pitted and chopped
2 teaspoons tomato paste

1 teaspoon garlic, minced
1 teaspoon capers, minced
160 ml (5½ fl oz) warm water
1 teaspoons salt
3 g (⅛ oz) fresh yeast

SUNFLOWER AND PINE NUT PANINO

230 g (8 oz) Manitoba flour
1 tablespoon sunflower seeds, toasted
1 tablespoon pine nuts, toasted
1 tablespoon pumpkin seeds, toasted

160 ml (5½ oz) warm water
1 teaspoon salt
3 g (⅛ oz) fresh yeast

HERB PANINO

230 g (8 oz) Manitoba flour
3 g (⅛ oz) fresh yeast
2 tablespoons mixed herbs (sage, thyme, rosemary, chives and marjoram), chopped finely

160 ml (5½ fl oz) warm water
1 teaspoon salt

In addition to the quantity of flour in the ingredients, set aside a small bowl of more flour for dusting. Combine the flour and flavouring ingredients in a bowl and make a well in the centre. In a separate bowl, mix the water, salt and yeast together. Add the liquid into the well and work with your hands to combine. Work the dough in a wave-like motion to incorporate air. When the texture and colour are even (about 1 minute), cover with plastic film and rest in a warm, dry place for 35 minutes. Sprinkle the surface of the dough with flour and 'turn' it by pulling small portions of the dough around the edge towards the opposite side of the bowl, covering and incorporating the flour. Once one full turn has been made, rest for 35 more minutes. Repeat the procedure two more times, resting for 35 minutes after each turn. While the dough is resting for the final time, preheat the oven to Gas Mark 9/250°C/480°F and heat a baking stone or sheet inside. On the bottom rack of the oven, place a small baking tin with a little water in it to produce steam. Hold the bowl at a tilt and gently pull out the dough onto a flat surface dusted with flour. Sprinkle more flour onto the surface of the dough and gently press with the back of your hands to spread it out. Use a pizza cutter to portion the dough into 12 miniature loaves. Rest for 10 minutes, covered with a clean cloth, then remove the hot stone or sheet from the oven and dust it with flour. Place the breads upside-down on the stone and bake for 8 minutes. Reduce the heat to Gas Mark 6/200°C/400°F and bake for 5 more minutes or until the breads are light. Remove from the oven and serve warm.

CIABATTA

This well known Italian bread literally translates to 'slipper' because of its long, flat shape. Ciabatta, soft and airy, must be eaten fresh.

1 loaf　(E)　*10 minutes & 115 minutes rising & 20 minutes baking*

INGREDIENTS*

460 g (1 lb) Manitoba flour, plus more for dusting

2 teaspoons salt

318 ml (10½ fl oz) warm water

6 g (¼ oz) fresh yeast

Place the flour in a large bowl and make a well in the centre. In a separate bowl, mix the salt, water and yeast together. Pour the liquid into the well and work with your hands to combine. Work the dough in a wave-like motion to incorporate air. When the colour and texture are smooth, cover with plastic film and rest in a warm, dry place for 35 minutes. Sprinkle the surface of the dough with flour and 'turn' it by pulling small portions of the dough around the edge towards the opposite side of the bowl, covering and incorporating the flour. Once one full turn has been made, rest for 35 more minutes. Repeat the procedure two more times, resting for 35 minutes after each turn. While the dough is resting for the final time, preheat the oven to Gas Mark 9/250°C/480°F and heat a baking stone or sheet inside. On the bottom rack of the oven, place a small baking tin with a little water in it to produce steam. Hold the bowl at a tilt and gently pull out the dough onto a flat surface dusted with flour. Sprinkle more flour onto the surface of the dough, gently pressing with the back of your hands to spread it out. Shape into a narrow loaf, cover with a clean cloth and rest for 10 minutes. Then remove the hot stone or sheet from the oven and dust it with more flour. Gently transfer the loaf, upside down, onto the sheet and bake for 12 minutes. Reduce the heat to Gas Mark 6/200°C/400°F and bake for an additional 8 minutes, or until the bread feels light. Remove from the oven and cool for a few minutes before slicing to serve.

*GLUTEN FREE CIABATTA CON FARINA DI CECI (CHICKPEA FLOUR)

115 g (4 oz) chickpea flour

115 g (4 oz) rice flour

8 g (⅓ oz) gluten free yeast

160 ml (5 fl oz) warm water

2 tablespoons chopped hazelnuts

2 tablespoons re-hydrated raisins

Salt to taste

Follow the same procedure as above.

*GLUTEN FREE CIABATTA ALLE NOCI (WALNUTS)

115 g (4 oz) cornflour

115 g (4 oz) rice flour

8 g (⅓ oz) gluten free yeast

160 ml (5 fl oz) warm water

4 tablespoons chopped walnuts

Salt to taste

Follow the same procedure as above.

FOCACCIA alle OLIVE

Similar to pizza bread, this soft, flat bread is mixed with olives.

1 loaf   E   *15 minutes & 80 minutes rising & 12 minutes baking*

INGREDIENTS

150 g (5½ oz) Manitoba flour, plus more for dusting

50 g (2 oz) Grano Duro flour

120 g (4½ oz) green and black olives, pitted and roughly chopped

1 tablespoon extra virgin olive oil, plus more for drizzling

125 ml (4½ fl oz) warm water

½ teaspoon salt

6 g (¼ oz) fresh yeast

Coarse sea salt

―――――

Combine the flours and olives in a bowl and make a well in the centre. In a separate bowl, mix the oil, water, salt and yeast together. Pour all the liquid into the well and work with your hands until the dough comes together. Work the dough in a circular, wave-like motion to incorporate air. When the texture and colour are even, drizzle the surface with olive oil and spread gently with your fingers. Cover with plastic film and rest in a warm, dry place for 35 minutes. Sprinkle the surface of the dough with flour and 'turn' it by pulling small portions of the dough around the edge towards the opposite side of the bowl. Once one full turn has been made, repeat two more times, starting by sprinkling more flour. Drizzle with more olive oil, spread with your fingers and rest for 35 more minutes.

Drizzle a baking sheet with 1½ tablespoons olive oil and spread around. Gently pull the dough from the bowl on to a flat surface dusted with flour. Roll out into a flat disc that is the width of the olives and transfer, as is, to the prepared sheet. Press down lightly with your fingertips all around the bread, creating indentations, and sprinkle coarse sea salt over the top. Cover with a clean cloth and rest for 10 minutes. Before baking, drizzle the surface with 1½ tablespoons olive oil and spread gently. Bake at Gas Mark 7/225°C/435°F for 12 minutes. Slice and serve warm.

For a delicious Rosemary Focaccia, replace the olives with 1 flat tablespoon of finely chopped rosemary. Before baking in the oven, sprinkle the surface with additional rosemary leaves.

PIZZA di PATATE

This 'white' pizza is an instant hit with children and adults alike. Roasted rosemary and sliced potatoes add a captivating, and addictive, flavour.

1 11-inch Pizza   Ⓔ   *20 minutes & 70 minutes rising & 12 minutes baking*

DOUGH

200 g (7 oz) Manitoba flour

55 g (2 oz) Grano Duro flour

1 tablespoon salt

6 g (¼ oz) fresh yeast

1 tablespoon olive oil

½ teaspoon sugar

125 ml (4 fl oz) warm water

———

Combine the flours in a bowl and form a well in the centre. In a separate bowl, mix the remaining ingredients together. Add the liquid into the well and work with your hands to combine. Work the dough in a wave-like motion to incorporate air. Add more water if too dry. When the texture is smooth (after about 1 minute of kneading) cover with plastic film and rest in a warm, dry place for 35 minutes. Sprinkle the surface of the dough with flour and 'turn' it by pulling small portions of the dough around the edge towards the opposite side of the bowl, covering and incorporating the flour. Once one full turn has been made, repeat two more times, starting by sprinkling more flour. Rest the dough for 35 more minutes.

TOPPING

1 small potato, peeled and thinly sliced with a mandolin

1 garlic clove, thinly sliced

Salt and black pepper to taste

1 tablespoon extra virgin olive oil, plus more for drizzling

1 teaspoon sea salt

1 sprig rosemary, stemmed

———

Toss the potato with the sliced garlic, salt, black pepper and 1 tablespoon of extra virgin olive oil.

ASSEMBLY

Preheat the oven to Gas Mark 7/225°C/430°F. Drizzle olive oil over a 23 x 33 cm (9 x 13") baking sheet. Remove the dough from the bowl and work around your wrists to open. Place on a lightly floured surface and roll out into a rectangle the size of the baking sheet. Transfer gently onto the prepared sheet. Overlap the potato slices on the dough, discarding the garlic slices in the process. Drizzle with olive oil and sprinkle coarse sea salt and rosemary over the top. Bake for 12–15 minutes or until the bottom of the pizza is brown and crunchy. Remove from the oven, drizzle over additional olive oil and serve.

PIZZA al POMODORO

Of all the different ways to make the most renowned pizza in the world, this dish will satisfy the most fussy gourmet.

1 11-inch Pizza (E) *20 minutes & 70 minutes rising & 12 minutes baking*

DOUGH

200 g (7 oz) Manitoba flour

55 g (2 oz) Grano Duro flour

1 tablespoon salt

6 g (¼ oz) fresh yeast

1 tablespoon olive oil

½ teaspoon sugar

125 ml (4 fl oz) warm water

———

Combine the flours in a bowl and form a well in the centre. In a separate bowl, mix the remaining ingredients together. Add the liquid into the well and work with your hands to combine. Work the dough in a wave-like motion to incorporate air. Add more water if too dry. When the texture is smooth (after about 1 minute of kneading) cover with plastic film and rest in a warm, dry place for 35 minutes. Sprinkle the surface of the dough with flour and 'turn' it by pulling small portions of the dough around the edge towards the opposite side of the bowl, covering and incorporating the flour. Once one full turn has been made, repeat two times, starting by sprinkling more flour. Rest for 35 more minutes.

TOPPING

½ quantity Tomato Sauce, at room temperature (see page 36)

1 tablespoon oregano

4 tablespoons grated Parmesan

5 basil leaves

112 g (4 oz) mozzarella, cut into 1 cm (½") cubes

Extra virgin olive oil, for drizzling

ASSEMBLY

Preheat the oven to Gas Mark 7/225°C/430°F. Drizzle olive oil over a 23 x 33 cm (9 x 13") baking sheet. Remove the dough from the bowl and work around your wrists to open. Place on a lightly floured surface and roll out into a rectangle the size of the baking sheet. Transfer gently into the prepared sheet. Pierce the surface with a fork to avoid air bubbles. Spread the Tomato Sauce over the dough and sprinkle with the oregano, Parmesan, basil leaves and mozzarella. Drizzle over olive oil. Bake for 12–15 minutes or until the bottom of the pizza is a toasty brown. Remove from the oven, slice and serve.

TORTA al TESTO

This famous round flatbread from Umbria is crunchy on the outside, soft in the middle and delicious eaten by itself or stuffed with a variety of foods. 'Testo' is the round-shaped pan on which the bread is cooked over the stove and was originally made from stone or terracotta and hung over a fire. Today, a testo is made of cast iron.

1 10-inch round   Ⓔ   *15 minutes & 70 minutes rising & 5 minutes baking*

DOUGH

200 g (7 oz) Manitoba flour

50 g (2 oz) Grano Duro flour

1½ tablespoons salt

6 g (¼ oz) fresh yeast

1 tablespoon olive oil

½ teaspoon sugar

125 ml (4 fl oz) warm water

———

Combine the flours in a bowl and form a well in the centre. In a separate bowl, mix the remaining ingredients together. Add the liquid into the well and work with your hands to combine. Work the dough in a wave-like motion to incorporate air. Add more water if too dry. When the texture is smooth (after about 1 minute of kneading) cover with plastic film and rest in a warm, dry place for 35 minutes. Sprinkle the surface of the dough with flour and 'turn' it by pulling small portions of the dough around the edge towards the opposite side of the bowl, covering and incorporating the flour. Once one full turn has been made, repeat twice, starting by sprinkling more flour. Rest for 35 more minutes.

TO SERVE

Preheat the oven to Gas Mark 7/220°C/430°F. Gently roll the ball of dough around your wrists to open into a rough 25 cm (10") disk and cover with a piece of cloth. Preheat the torta pan and sprinkle with flour. When the flour begins to brown, dust off the flour and place the dough on top. Pierce the surface with a fork and cook until one side is browned. Carefully flip with a metal spatula and cook on the other side. Transfer to the hot oven and bake for 5 minutes.

Serve as it is in wedges, or halve horizontally and stuff with fillings such as buffalo mozzarella, rocket and Parmesan. Cover with the top half and bake for 3 minutes more at Gas Mark 4/ 180°C/350°F.

PIZZA RUSTICA al FORMAGGIO

The term 'rustico' is most commonly used in southern Italy and signifies a savoury dish made of cheese. This soft bread is perfect by itself or alongside a light lunch of grilled vegetables and soup.

Serves 12   (E)   *20 minutes & 40 minutes rising & 15 minutes baking*

INGREDIENTS*

Extra virgin olive oil, for drizzling

Fine breadcrumbs

300 g (11 oz) Italian '00' flour

70 g (2½ oz) grated Parmesan

250 g (9 oz) Scamorza, cut into 1 cm (¼") cubes

1 teaspoon salt

100 g (3½ oz) melted butter

120 ml (4 fl oz) warm water

25 g (1 oz) fresh yeast

1 teaspoon sugar

3 eggs

———

Lightly grease a 23 x 13 cm (9 x 5") baking sheet with olive oil and dust with fine breadcrumbs. In a medium-sized bowl, combine the flour, cheeses, salt and melted butter. In a separate bowl or cup, mix together the warm water, yeast and sugar. Add to the flour mixture. Separately beat the eggs with a fork to break the yolks, then add to the flour and liquid mixture. Mix all ingredients together with one hand, using a wide circular motion to incorporate air into the dough. Continue with the circular motion for 30 seconds. Transfer to the prepared sheet and level out the dough with a spatula. Cover with a clean cloth and set aside for 40 minutes, or until the dough has doubled in size. Bake at Gas Mark 4/175°C/350°F for 15 minutes. Serve hot out of the oven.

*VEGAN ALTERNATIVE

100 g (3½ oz) Italian '00' flour

40 g (1½ oz) margarine

80 g (3 oz) tofu, cut into tiny cubes

10 g (⅓ oz) fresh yeast

3 tablespoons soy milk

3 tablespoons warm water

Salt to taste

———

Follow the same procedure as above.

There exists in this world a precarious, confined space full of razor-sharp edges, blistering fires and thousands of inflammable objects in close proximity. Those who subject themselves to this environment are machines: highly caffeinated workaholics who operate on autopilot. They expertly navigate the system, skilfully avoiding collisions and catastrophe everyday. They are the chefs of Montali, and this is their kitchen.

Unfortunately, no amount of culinary training or experience can thwart all accidents, mistakes and random acts of nature that occur in every restaurant. From minor cuts and burns to complete obliteration of a course minutes before it is to be served, the Country House Montali has had its fair share of debacles. Most incidences are laughable in retrospect and, even if the outcome was not positive, a valuable lesson was always learned.

The accidents

In the life of a chef, cuts and burns are the norm. Especially for a young apprentice, the only way to stop hurting oneself is to learn from many, many stupid mistakes. In some instances, however, the injury is not self-inflicted.

Ten minutes into dinner, all of the guests had been served their wine and were anxiously awaiting their antipasti. In the kitchen, Malu and another chef stood side-by-side frying batches of the mozzarella and tomato stuffed calzoni. "Be careful when you put the calzoni in the oil!" Malu advised. "It might splash." While she was saying this, the calzoni in her hand slipped out of her fingers and plopped into the oil like a brick. A long splatter of hot oil flew out of the pan and streaked the other chef's hand. Malu gasped and ran to get burn cream from the back while the stunned chef exhaled through the white-hot pain. Malu reappeared in a matter of seconds. "Excuse me! Oh, I'm so sorry!" she apologised while applying the cream to the burn. After a second, the other chef burst out

laughing, easing Malu's guilt. The irony of the situation was too comical to get upset over a minor burn. In reality, Malu is more likely to be the solution to a dilemma rather than the source.

The mistakes

In dealing with a crisis, the ability to handle problems coolly and effectively separates the professional from the amateur. On occasion, the chefs have had to create brand new dishes on the fly, minutes before they were set to serve dinner, due to another's colossal mistake.

On a day when Malu was up to her ears with errands, Maria stepped in to save the day. "Malu," she said confidently, "you go and run your errands. I'll take care of the kitchen." "Are you sure? You can think about today's dishes?" Malu asked her.

"No problem! It's under control. Go ahead," Maria responded. She loved feeling needed. So Malu left, leaving the kitchen in Maria's hands. She went to drop off the laundry, grab a few supplies, buy cases of wine and pick up her son from school. By the time she came back, it was half past five and she threw on her apron to prepare the evening's dessert.

Maria was working happily when Malu walked in and said, "Maria! I'm back. I'll start on the dolce."

"Don't worry, Malu. I've already done it! You relax!" Maria said proudly.

"Really? Wonderful!" On her command, Malu went back upstairs to work on the following day's menu and spend time with Damiano. At 7.30 pm, she returned to the kitchen. During dinner, she and Maria were getting ready for the antipasti when Malu casually asked Maria where the secondi was. Maria paused to think for a minute before her eyes bulged and jaw dropped. Without a word, Malu knew exactly what had happened: Maria had completely forgotten to make the secondi.

Leaving Maria to finish serving, Malu threw open the refrigerator and scanned the contents, pulling out various ingredients. Working like a maniac, she chopped courgettes, red peppers, onions and tomatoes and sautéed them over a high fire, finishing them off with chopped parsley and basil. She grilled large seitan patties, originally prepared for the following day's dinner, with mixed vegetables before slicing them very thinly horizontally. She patted each slice with flour, dipped them in an egg wash, and then breaded all sides before frying them to a golden brown in a sauté pan. Malu layered the sautéed vegetables between three levels of crunchy

seitan in a large baking dish, sprinkled assorted grated cheeses on top, cooked it in the oven until the surface was bubbly, and served it to delighted guests right away. A thoroughly embarrassed Maria apologized profusely to Malu who, seeing as how Maria was punishing herself enough, chose to console rather than lecture her.

More than other head chefs, Malu has patience for mistakes. She will laugh at the minor things like a dropped plate here or a river of spilled cream there, putting the guilt-ridden offender at ease. However, if the same person continues to make the same errors in judgement and repeat mistakes, her patience will wear thin.

Several years ago, a young local girl named Marcella was hired to help in the kitchen and dining room. She was proud and arrogant and intensely disliked being told what to do. Because she did not put any thought into her actions, she became notorious for dropping, spilling, burning and ruining materials around the kitchen. One evening, Malu had her hands full and called Marcella over. "Marcella, can you go to the back fridge to get the chocolate cake? It's on the second shelf, but be very careful when you pull it out."

"Yes, okay," Marcella replied half-heartedly, her gaze elsewhere.

"Marcella, you have to be very careful when you pull the cake out. It's very large and difficult to carry," Malu continued, insisting on eye contact with the girl. Marcella nodded vacantly and went to get the cake. The back room is attached to the main kitchen and only a step away, so when Marcella did not return after three minutes, Malu began to worry. "Luciana," she said, "can you please go check on Marcella?" Luciana stepped out of the kitchen and into the back. When she returned, the shock on her face gave her away.

Malu stormed to the back where Marcella was hovering over a chocolate explosion that was once a rich cake. She had dropped the dolce.

Marcella's mistake was not due to an accidental memory lapse, as was the case with Maria, it was caused by habitual incompetence. Malu absolutely let her have it. For a good five minutes, she ripped into Marcella relentlessly until the young girl was reduced to tears, finally feeling remorseful. After Malu finished projecting her frustrations on Marcella, she ran around the kitchen to prepare some sort of dessert for the guests. She managed to serve them a version of the Fragole con Zabaione e Crema, using mixed chopped fruits instead of strawberries. Marcella spent two more weeks at Montali until both parties decided the work was not for her.

The random acts of nature

In the later months of the season, torrential thunderstorms frequent the Umbrian countryside. The Country House Montali has had its fair share of blackouts and floods, the effects of which could have been terrible for the restaurant.

The benefit of having a staff that works, lives, eats and sleeps at Montali is that their creative minds can run the kitchen like clockwork, even in the dark.

"Alberto, the lights went off again," Sang said to Alberto, as if the fact that the kitchen had gone pitch black was not a clear indication already.

Alberto walked over to the circuit board to flip the switches, which usually turns the lights back on immediately. When it did not work, he tried it another time. Then another time. He gave it a few seconds and tried yet again. After the eighth time, he cursed. It was four in the afternoon and the chefs were still in the middle of preparing dinner.

"There's no electricity," he announced as he walked back into the kitchen. "What's the situation on tonight's dinner?" "We still have to prepare the Strudel di Zucchine! And the bread has to be baked," one chef nervously responded. The oven was completely out and the Strudel, a pastry encased courgette roulade, had not even been started.

"Va bene," Malu said. "No problem, we'll just change the secondi!" She racked her brain for ideas, but the only secondi that did not require an oven had been served the previous night. Hiding her anxiety from the other chefs, she breathed deeply and said, "We invent a new one today!" She sat down with Sang and Janko and, collaboratively, they decided to make mixed grilled vegetable and fruit skewers, which later became Spiedini Primavera, a favourite among guests. With the use of the gas stove, they replaced the standard ciabatta with a thin whole wheat torta al testo stuffed with rocket and thin slices of Parmigiano Reggiano. Rather than making the Soufflé di Ricotta that required the oven, they made Budino al Cocco, a Brazilian coconut pudding with a rich plum sauce.

Because the water pump was electric, they took turns running to the well in the rain to draw water for cooking.

That evening, guests were served in the romantically lit dining room full of candles.

Without a thought to how the sumptuous dinner had been prepared, the guests raved about it. In the kitchen, the exhausted chefs burst out laughing. The laughter stopped though at the thought of the breakfast preparation next morning, as the evening meal had produced dozen of dirty pans and plates that couldn't be washed for lack of water. Great was their relief to see lights popping on again, solving that last problem.

In another storm-induced incident, the guests were not only fully aware of the problem, they were a huge part of the solution. Years before, Malu and Alberto had had electrical wires built underground extending one kilometre past their restaurant so that they would not be visible and unsightly. The installation of the wires created an underground channel through which, Malu and Alberto later found, water could flow.

During the last of four cookery courses with two hilarious English couples, Malu was rolling umbricelli noodles when one of them pointed to the dining room and exclaimed, "The restaurant is flooded!" Malu glanced over and saw that an enormous quantity of water had flowed from the outside and into the restaurant. (Later, they discovered that the water had travelled through the electrical channel and through the circuit box attached to the dining room.)

Malu called Alberto, dropped everything, threw off her apron and they both ran to the dining room. The four students cheerfully kicked off their shoes and joined in to help them move furniture from the flooded areas. Soaking the water up with towels and draining it into buckets, they managed to get rid of most of the water, wash their hands and return to their lesson.

At dinner a few hours later, they merrily recounted the story to the other restaurant guests who rolled with laughter. At the end of dinner, all of the guests were sitting in the lounge sipping drinks with Alberto when one of the chefs in the kitchen noticed that the restaurant floor looked strange. Taking a closer look, he realized that it had flooded yet again, but this time the water was ankle deep. As soon as Malu and Alberto came to look, they ran to call the fire department.

"I'm sorry," said the fireman on the phone, "but we cannot drain your restaurant until the water is at least 20 centimetres high. Our draining machine will not operate." "What should I do, then? Flood my restaurant with more water so that you'll come?" Alberto inquired.

"Listen, we can put you on the list and try to come out there tonight, but there is no guarantee when we can come. The entire area is in the same situation you are in, if not worse." The restaurant patrons, when they heard the news, jumped up at the chance to be part of the action. "We'll help!" they exclaimed. For the next two hours, everyone went to work draining the restaurant in the same manner as before, soaking themselves completely in the process.

As the last towel was wrung out, the entrance doors to the restaurant swung open and three burly firemen with their hands on their hips said quite heroically, "We're here!" There was an eruption of laughter as Alberto made his way over to them. Close up, he could see that they were exhausted from following one emergency after another all over northern Umbria. He put his hand on one man's shoulders and invited them in. Alberto distributed glasses to everyone and opened several bottles of wine that night as the guests and firemen sat in the front lobby and laughed the night away.

Although none of the mishaps over the past 20 years are experiences Malu or Alberto would like to go through again, from them they have countless stories and rich memories. They are imprints of the people that they have shared their lives with and add to the character with which the restaurant and hotel were built. Accidents will happen, mistakes will be made and fierce storms will pass through for as long as the Country House Montali stands. But as long as Malu, Alberto and their carefully selected staff are there, they will welcome the challenge.

Dolci

DESSERTS

DOCINHOS di COCO

These chewy, caramel-like Brazilian candies melt in your mouth. For variety, dip the chocolate sweets in coconut flakes, and the coconut sweets in the chocolate flakes.

100 of each   Ⓔ   *60 minutes*

BRIGADEIROS

400 g (14 oz) sweetened condensed milk

2 tablespoons butter, plus more for greasing

2 tablespoons unsweetened cocoa powder

70 g (2½ oz) chocolate sprinkles, for coating

———

Combine the condensed milk, butter and cocoa in a saucepan and mix well. Cook over a low heat, stirring continuously, until the mixture begins to pull away from the bottom of the pan. Cook for an additional 5 minutes, then remove from the heat. Transfer onto a buttered ceramic plate to cool. When at room temperature, roll teaspoon-sized portions into a ball between your buttered palms. Drop into a bowl filled with chocolate sprinkles and roll until coated. Set aside on a plate and refrigerate.

BEIJINHOS DI COCO

1 medium coconut, grated

400 g (14 fl oz) sweetened condensed milk

2 egg yolks

2 tablespoons butter

½ vanilla stick, halved lengthwise and scraped

70 g (2½ oz) coconut flakes, for coating

Cloves for studding (optional)

———

Combine the coconut, condensed milk, egg yolks, butter and vanilla in a saucepan and mix well. Cook over a low heat, stirring continuously, until the mixture begins to pull away from the bottom of the pan. Continue to cook until the bottom starts to colour slightly. Transfer onto a buttered ceramic plate to cool. When at room temperature, roll teaspoon-sized portions into a ball between your buttered palms. Drop into a bowl filled with coconut flakes and roll until coated. Stud each ball with a clove if desired. Set aside on a plate and refrigerate.

OLHO DI SOGRA *(Mother in law's eye)*

1 medium coconut, grated

400 ml (14 fl oz) sweetened condensed milk

½ vanilla stick, halved lengthwise and scraped

2 tablespoons butter

2 egg yolks

1 bag prunes, slit and
    stone removed

———

Follow the same procedure as the Beijinhos di Coco but, rather than rolling in coconut flakes, press each small ball of mixture into a prune so that each is the shape of a big 'eye'.

Arrange these beautiful sweets on a nice white tray, alternating the black and white colours to bring an added elegance to any party.

DELIZIA AL LIMONE

A soft, spongy lemon delight, typical of Campania and the Amalfi coast. Don't forget to keep the Limoncello in the freezer.

Serves 6   (M)   *55 minutes*

CAKE

2 eggs, yolks and whites separated

50 g (1¾ oz) sugar

½ teaspoon vanilla extract

Pinch of salt

28 g (1 oz) flour

1 teaspoon baking powder

Zest of ½ lemon

———

Butter and flour six ramekins. Line the bottoms with parchment paper. Preheat the oven to Gas Mark 2/150°C/300°F. Beat the egg yolks, sugar and vanilla until pale yellow. Beat the egg whites and salt with a mixer to stiff peaks. Gently fold the whites into the yolks in two batches. Sift in the flour and baking powder and fold in the lemon zest. Divide the batter between the ramekins and place on a baking tray. Bake for 25 minutes. Remove from the oven and cool.

PASTRY CREAM

180 ml (6 fl oz) milk

25 g (1 oz) lemon juice

½ vanilla bean, split and scraped

3 egg yolks

50 g (1¾ oz) sugar

28 g (1 oz) flour

Rind of ½ lemon

———

Heat the milk, lemon rind and vanilla over a medium heat. In a separate saucepan, whisk the egg yolks and sugar until pale yellow. Add the flour and continue to whisk well until combined. As soon as the milk comes to a boil, take off the heat and pour into the yolk mixture, whisking all the time. Cook this cream over a double boiler over a medium heat, stirring, for 4 minutes or until thickened. Remove from the heat and cool over an ice bath (see page 21). Discard the lemon rind and vanilla and add the lemon juice. Mix well. Refrigerate, covered.

BAGNA (SOAKING SAUCE)

100 ml (3¼ fl oz) water

28 g (1 oz) sugar

60 g (2 fl oz) Limoncello

———

Mix the water and sugar in a saucepan until boiling. Remove from the heat and cool. Add the Limoncello.

ASSEMBLY

When the cakes have cooled, run a knife around the edges of the ramekin cups and remove the cakes. Cut out a small circle from the bottom of each cake and set aside. Using a piping bag, fill each cake with the pastry cream. Replace the cut-out circles and place the cakes, cut-side up, on a tray. Pour the sauce over the cakes to soak, cover with plastic film and refrigerate. Reserve any leftover pastry cream.

TO SERVE

240 ml (8 fl oz) double cream

1 tablespoon icing sugar

90 g (3 fl oz) Limoncello

Lemon Strings (see page 29)

——

Beat the double cream with the icing sugar to soft peaks, then fold two-thirds into the leftover pastry cream. Add the Limoncello and mix. Place the cakes on individual serving plates, cut-side down, and cover with this cream. Top with a dollop of whipped cream, garnish with a few lemon strings and serve immediately.

TIRAMISU

TIRAMISU – how it should be!

Serves 8 Ⓔ *40 minutes & 2 hours chilling*

INGREDIENTS

90 ml (3 fl oz) brewed espresso, cold

1½ teaspoon of Grand Marnier, Maraschino and Marsala, mixed

3 tablespoons granulated sugar, plus 1 tablespoon for the espresso

2 eggs, whites and yolks separated

100 g (3½ oz) mascarpone

1 pinch salt

80 ml (2½ fl oz) double cream

1 teaspoon icing sugar

70 g (2½ oz) Pavesini biscuits

2 tablespoons grated bittersweet chocolate

½ tablespoon cocoa powder, for dusting

———

Mix the espresso, liqueurs, and 1 tablespoon sugar together until the sugar has dissolved. Set aside and cool.

Whisk the 3 tablespoons of sugar with the egg yolks in a large bowl until foamy and pale in color. Fold in the mascarpone. With a hand-held mixer, beat the egg whites with salt to stiff peaks.

In separate bowl, whip the double cream and icing sugar with a handheld mixer until the cream can hold its shape and is no longer liquid. Gently fold into the yolk mixture.

Fold the egg whites into the yolk mixture, using a gentle, wave-like motion.

ASSEMBLY

Use a small, rimmed serving dish or a 10 cm (4") glass bowl. Pour a quarter of the egg mixture into the bottom and level with a spoon. Soak a third of the Pavesini biscuits in the coffee mixture, remove and drain the excess liquid back into the espresso. Lay the biscuits in the serving dish. Repeat the layering process, alternating between biscuits and cream. Finish with cream, sprinkle with grated bittersweet chocolate and refrigerate for 2 hours. Immediately before serving, powder the top of the Tiramisu with cocoa powder. Enjoy!

The literal translation for this delectable favourite is 'pull me up'. The tale of the dessert's origins begins over 300 years ago in Siena with a visit to the medieval city by Grand Duke Cosimo de' Medici III. Bearing in mind his renowned sweet tooth, Sienese chefs created a delectable layer cake they named 'Zuppa del Duca', or 'Duke's Soup'.

Thoroughly enjoying the dessert, the Grand Duke took the recipe with him to Florence to introduce it to the upper crust of Tuscan society. Over 100 years later the dessert became wildly popular among English intellectuals and, for a short time, it was renamed 'Zuppa Inglese'.

In Italy, the dessert continued in popularity and spread to Treviso, northwest of Venice. Rumour has it that the Venetian courtesans made a point of eating this dessert before business affairs, thus the new name, 'Tira-mi-su.'

STRUDEL di MELE

Apple strudel. The Austro-Hungarian empire left behind this famous dish, which has been adopted by the northern provinces of Italy bordering Austria. This pastry, the glory of the city of Vienna, has always been a very handy one, as it can be filled with a sweet or savoury filling.

Serves 12　**D**　*50 minutes & 15 minutes rising*

FILLING

4 tablespoons breadcrumbs

2 tablespoons butter, melted

3 apples, peeled, cored and sliced into 2 mm (⅛") pieces

5 apricots, peeled, cored and sliced slightly thicker than the apples

100 g (3½ oz) raisins, re-hydrated with sherry and drained

55 g (2 oz) almonds, roasted and chopped

28 g (1 oz) pine nuts, toasted and left whole

2 tablespoons brown sugar

1 teaspoon ground cinnamon

Zest of 1 lemon

Zest of 1 orange

1 teaspoon lemon juice

2 tablespoons apricot jam or marmalade

———

Toast the breadcrumbs in the melted butter until golden brown, cool and set aside. Mix the other filling ingredients together in a large bowl.

DOUGH

250 g (9 oz) Italian '00' flour

125 ml (4 fl oz) water, room temperature

50 g (1½ oz) butter, cubed and at room temperature

Pinch of salt

45 ml (1½ oz) single cream, for brushing

———

Sift the flour onto a flat surface. Make a well in the centre, add the water, butter and salt and work with your fingers until a dough begins to form. Knead for 30 seconds, then forcefully throw the dough down onto the surface 100 times. Cover with a warm glass bowl for 15 minutes (the glass bowl can be briefly heated in a warm oven).

ASSEMBLY

Flour a clean cloth. Shape the dough into a disc and slowly roll over your wrists to open. When it begins to thin (but not break), place on the cloth and gently pull into a rectangular shape, approximately 46 x 25 cm (18 x 10"), maintaining the thickness. The dough should be slightly transparent and as large and thin as possible. Trim the edges with a pizza cutter. Brush cream over the surface and sprinkle with the toasted breadcrumbs. Dot filling evenly over the crumbs, leaving a 1 cm (½") margin at the top edge uncovered. Using the cloth as a guide, fold in the sides. Pull the cloth up from the bottom corners and gently roll up the strudel. Continue to roll the strudel on to a sheet of parchment paper until the seam side is down. Brush the surface with more cream. Transfer, with the parchment paper, on to a baking sheet. Bake at Gas Mark 4/180°C/350°F for 40 minutes or until golden. Slice and serve warm, dusted with icing sugar and a dollop of whipped cream.

VULCANO di CIOCCOLATO

A chocolate volcano cake served with a liquorice ice cream and kiwi sauce. A great way to end an important dinner. The hot and cold contrast is a pleasant suprise.

Serves 8 Ⓜ *30 minutes & 2 hours freezing*

CAKE

150 g (5½ oz) 70% bittersweet chocolate, chopped

140 g (5 oz) butter

100 g (3½ oz) sugar

3 whole eggs, at room temperature

1 egg yolk, at room temperature

1 pinch of salt

40 g (1½ oz) flour

Grease and flour eight ramekins and line with a small piece of parchment paper. Heat the chocolate, butter and sugar in a double boiler over simmering water until completely melted. Cool to room temperature. Beat the eggs and salt until frothy and whisk into the chocolate. (Note: It is important that the chocolate and eggs, when combined, are the same temperature so that the chocolate does not solidify). Sift in the flour and mix quickly until just combined. Divide the batter among the ramekins, cover with foil and freeze for at least 2 hours.

LIQUORICE GELATO

½ teaspoon natural liquorice candies, finely chopped

180 g (6 fl oz) double cream

300 ml (10 fl oz) milk

75 g (2½ oz) sugar

Combine all the ingredients in a double boiler over a low heat. Stir until the liquorice melts completely. Pour through a fine sieve to catch any remaining solid particles. Cool over an ice bath (see page 21) and pass through a fine sieve a second time. Whisk to foam lightly. Pour into an ice cream or gelato machine. Store the resulting ice cream in an air-tight container in the freezer for up to 1 week.

KIWI SAUCE

4 kiwi fruit

Icing sugar to taste

1 teaspoon lemon juice

Purée the ingredients together in a blender. Pour through a sieve and reserve the sauce.

TO SERVE

Preheat the oven to Gas Mark 9/250°C/480°F. Place the ramekins on a baking tray, uncovered and bake for 7–8 minutes, or until the cakes feel crunchy on the outside but are still soft in the centre. With a towel in each hand, carefully remove each individual cake and place, right side up, on a plate. Dust with icing sugar and a pinch of chilli powder. Serve hot with a drizzle of Kiwi Sauce and Liquorice Gelato.

It is crucial that all cake ingredients, when mixed together, are at the same temperature. If not, the chocolate may seize and become brittle. This dessert can stay in the freezer, unbaked, for up to 2 weeks.

TORTA di LIMONE

Lemon pie. The refreshing lemony filling is surrounded by a soft pastry. Ideal for afternoon tea. Great with Carrot Sorbet.

Serves 16　Ⓜ　*50 minutes & chilling time*

FILLING

300 ml (10 fl oz) water, at room temperature

200 g (7 oz) sugar

50 g (1¾ oz) cornflour

Zest of 3 lemons

1 egg

Juice of 2 lemons

─────

Whisk the water, sugar, cornflour and lemon zest together in a saucepan. Bring to a boil. Cook for 1 minute then remove from the heat to cool completely before adding in the egg and lemon juice. Mix well and set aside.

DOUGH

150 g (5 oz) sugar

400 g (14¼ oz) Italian '00' flour

150 g (5 oz) butter, at room temperature

2 eggs

1 tablespoon Marsala wine

1 tablespoon lemon juice

2 teaspoons baking powder

─────

On a flat surface, combine the sugar with the flour and make a well in the centre. Add the remaining ingredients into the well and work with your fingertips until a dough begins to form. Incorporate by cutting through the dough with a pastry cutter and rolling back together, three or four times, until the texture and colour are even. Wrap in plastic film and refrigerate for 15 minutes.

Roll two-thirds of the dough between two sheets of floured parchment paper into a round disc 33 cm (13") in diameter. Remove the top layer of parchment paper and gently invert the dough over an 28 cm (11") tart tin. Gently press the dough into the bottom, edges and sides. Pour in the lemon filling and spread evenly with a spatula. Open the remaining dough in the same manner into a disc just big enough to cover the lemon filling. Invert over the filling and seal the edges of the dough. Cut off excess dough with a small knife or pie cutter. Bake at Gas Mark 4/180°C/350°F for 25 minutes. Cool to room temperature and chill in the refrigerator.

TO SERVE

Carefully remove the tart from the tin, slice into wedges, dust with icing sugar and serve with a scoop of Carrot Sorbet (see page 279).

TORTA di CIOCCOLATO e NOCI

Chocolate and nut cake. A blend of soft melting flavours that you can enjoy at any time or even use as a base for a birthday cake with a chocolate ganache topping.

Serves 12   E   *20 minutes & 25 minutes baking & cooling time*

INGREDIENTS

Butter and flour for dusting

4 eggs, whites and yolks separated

200 g (7 oz) sugar

2 drops vanilla extract

1 pinch salt

100 g (3½ oz) walnuts, chopped

100 g (3½ oz) almonds, chopped

200 g (7 oz) bittersweet chocolate, chopped

———

Line a spring-form 28 cm (11") tart tin with parchment paper. Butter and flour the surface. Preheat the oven to Gas Mark 4/175°C/350°F. Whisk the egg yolks, sugar and vanilla together until pale yellow and frothy. Using a mixer, whisk the egg whites with the salt to stiff peaks. Gently fold the two egg mixtures together. Fold in the nuts and chocolate in four batches and immediately pour into the tin. Using a spatula, gently smooth out the top, then bake for 25 minutes. Remove from the oven and set aside to cool completely. Serve at room temperature with a dusting of icing sugar and a generous dollop of whipped cream. (For a gluten-free version, leave out the dusting flour, using parchment paper as an alternative.)

PERE COTTE al VINO BIANCO

Pears cooked in spiced white wine. Present this elegant dish with a drizzle of Cinnamon Pastry Cream and Chocolate Sauce.

Serves 8 E *40 minutes & cooling time*

PEARS

1 lemon	1 cinnamon stick
1 orange	5 cloves
500 ml (16 fl oz) white wine	8 Bartlett pears, peeled
100 g (3½ oz) sugar	

Peel the rind from the lemon and orange in large pieces. Combine it with the wine, sugar, cinnamon and cloves in a pot and bring to a boil. As soon as it comes to a boil, reduce to a simmer and add the whole pears. Cover and cook over a low heat for 30 minutes or until cooked through. The pears, when pierced with a toothpick, should offer no resistance. Cool completely, strain the sauce and set aside the wine sauce and pears separately.

CINNAMON PASTRY CREAM

1 egg yolk	1½ tablespoons sugar
1 tablespoon butter, chilled	Cinnamon to taste

Combine the egg yolk, butter and sugar in a double boiler and cook over simmering water, stirring continuously, for 3 minutes or until thickened. Add cinnamon to taste and cool.

CHOCOLATE SAUCE

200 g (7 oz) bittersweet chocolate	150 ml (5¼ fl oz) double cream

Grate the chocolate and melt with the cream over a double boiler, mixing well. When smooth, remove from the heat and cool to room temperature. Pour into a squeezy bottle. To reheat, place the bottle in a bowl filled with hot water, being careful not to let the water go inside the tip.

TO SERVE

Reheat the chocolate sauce. Halve the pears lengthwise, then slice each half thinly, starting 5 mm (¼") from the stem (see picture). Press gently so that the slices, kept intact at the stem, lean on a slant. Spoon the cream on to individual plates and place one pear on the cream. Drizzle with the reserved wine sauce. Pour over chocolate sauce and serve.

PESCHE RIPIENE

Stuffed peaches. Amaretti biscuits provide a bitter almond taste that combines with the chocolate and the fresh peaches perfectly. To be made when the best quality peaches are available. The best are the ones that easily 'break' in half.

Serves 6   (E)   *10 minutes & 25 minutes baking*

INGREDIENTS

6 firm peaches

Brown sugar

———

Wash and split the peaches in half. Remove the stones and scoop out the flesh with a melon baller, leaving 5 mm (¼") all round the edge. Reserve the peach flesh. Place the peach halves, cut-side up, on a baking tray lined with parchment paper. Sprinkle the insides with brown sugar.

FILLING

45 g (1½ oz) hazelnuts, chopped

45 g (1½ oz) bittersweet chocolate, at least 43% cocoa

12 amaretti biscuits, coarsely ground

1 tablespoon Amaretto liqueur (such as di Saronno)

1 teaspoon lemon juice

12 whole hazelnuts

3 tablespoons brown sugar

———

Chop the reserved peach flesh well and mix with the remaining filling ingredients except the whole hazelnuts and sugar. Divide the filling among the peach halves. Top each with one hazelnut, sprinkle additional brown sugar on the top and bake at Gas Mark 4/180°C/350°F for 25 minutes. Serve at room temperature.

CAFFÉ BRULÉE

A soft creamy coffee custard with crunchy caramelised brown sugar on top. An excellent dessert to keep you going. Remember you can also use decaffeinated coffee.

Serves 5   (E)   *25 minutes & 1 hour cooking & 4 hours chilling*

INGREDIENTS

75 g (2⅔ oz) sugar

5 egg yolks

1 tablespoon instant espresso

500 ml (16 fl oz) double cream

6 teaspoons granulated brown sugar

———

Whisk the sugar and egg yolks together in a bowl until frothy and well incorporated. In a separate pan, dissolve the espresso in the cream over heat. As soon as it comes to a boil, remove from the heat. Pour into the egg mixture, whisking all the time so not to scramble the eggs. Pour through a sieve and carefully pour into ramekins or oven-proof coffee cups. Carefully transfer the cups on to a baking tray with 5 cm (2") sides. Skim foam and bubbles from the surfaces with a spoon. Fill the baking tray halfway up the sides of the ramekins with boiling water and cover with foil. Bake at Gas Mark 2/150°C/300°F for 1 hour. Remove from the oven, take the ramekins out of the water and cool to room temperature before refrigerating for at least 4 hours.

COOKIES

15 g (½ oz) icing sugar

15 g (½ oz) egg whites

15 g (½ oz) butter, melted and cooled to room temperature

15 g (½ oz) flour

———

Preheat the oven to Gas Mark 4/180°C/350°F. Beat the sugar with the egg whites and mix in the melted butter. Sift in the flour and whisk well. Grease a Silpat (a silicon tray) and dust with flour. For each cookie, evenly spread 1 tablespoon of batter into a 10 cm (4") circle on the Silpat. Bake for 2 minutes or until golden brown. Remove from the oven and use a small spatula to transfer the cookies to a tray lined with paper towels. Cool completely.

TO SERVE

Sprinkle 1 teaspoon of brown sugar over the surface of the custard and tap the sides to disperse the sugar evenly. Caramelise the surface with a hand-held blow torch and serve immediately, topping with a cookie.

MOUSSE di CIOCCOLATO

This delightful chocolate mousse is airy in texture, rich in taste and goes perfectly with strawberries served at the peak of their season.

Serves 5 Ⓜ *50 minutes & 4 hours chilling*

MOUSSE

100 g (3½ oz) bittersweet chocolate, 43% cocoa, grated

3 egg yolks, at room temperature

300 ml (10 fl oz) double cream, at room temperature

———

Melt the chocolate in a double boiler. Remove from the heat and cool to room temperature. Beat the egg yolks and mix thoroughly with the chocolate. Whip the double cream to soft peaks with a hand-held mixer and fold in to the chocolate until just combined. Cover and refrigerate for at least 4 hours.

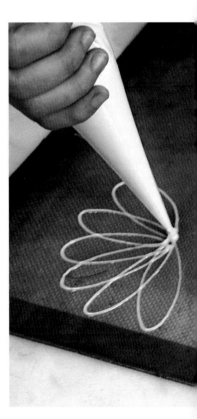

STRAWBERRY SAUCE

20 strawberries, stems removed

White wine, for rinsing fruit

4 tablespoons sugar

2 tablespoons cassis liqueur

———

Gently rinse the strawberries in white wine. Quarter six strawberries and set aside. Purée the remaining in a blender. Strain the liquid through a fine sieve. Mix with the sugar and cassis. Cover the sauce and set aside.

COOKIES (OPTIONAL)

15 g (½ oz) egg whites

15 g (½ oz) icing sugar

15 g (½ oz) butter, melted and cooled to room temperature

15 g (½ oz) flour

———

Preheat the oven to Gas Mark 4/180°C/350°F. Mix the cookie ingredients together until completely smooth. Pour into a piping bag with a fine tip. Line a wide baking tray with greased parchment paper or grease a Silpat (a silicon tray). Delicately pipe out the batter into the shape of a flower with overlapping petals, approximately 13 cm (5") in diameter or slightly wider than the rim of a martini glass. Bake in the oven for 1–2 minutes or until golden-brown. Remove from the oven and use a small spatula or butter knife to gently remove the delicate cookies while still hot and soft. Lay completely flat on a tray lined with paper towels.

TO SERVE

Scoop the chilled mousse into a piping bag with a large star tip and pipe out into Martini glasses. Line four strawberry quarters around the rim, cut-side down, and drizzle the strawberry sauce around the sides. Serve with a cookie leaning on the side of the Martini glass.

SEMIFREDDO DI MELE

A 'simple' apple pudding is heavenly when transformed by the subtle touch of cinnamon, vanilla and lemon in this 'semi-cold' dessert. Enjoy on a cold winter night with a glass of spicy red wine by the fire.

Serves 6   Ⓔ   *20 minutes & 2 hours chilling*

PASTRY CREAM*

500 ml (16 fl oz) milk

Rind of ½ lemon

½ vanilla bean, split and scraped

4 tablespoons sugar

4 egg yolks

4 tablespoons flour

———

Bring the milk, lemon rind and vanilla to a boil, then turn off the heat. Meanwhile, in a medium-sized saucepan, whisk the sugar with the egg yolks until pale yellow. Sift in the flour and mix well. Discard the lemon rind and vanilla from the milk and pour all the milk into the egg mixture, whisking all the time. Cook this cream in a double boiler over a medium heat for 3 minutes or until thickened. Cool over an ice bath (see page 21). Cover with plastic film so that the film touches the surface of the cream (to prevent a skin from forming). Set aside.

APPLES

5 Granny Smith apples

Juice of ½ lemon

1 tablespoon sugar

½ cinnamon stick

Rind of ½ lemon

———

Peel and core the apples. Slice thinly on a mandolin or by hand. Squeeze the lemon juice over the apples to prevent browning. Cook with the sugar, cinnamon stick and lemon rind in a small pot over a low heat, covered. Stir occasionally. Remove from the heat when the apples begin to caramelise, about 5 minutes. Remove the cinnamon and lemon rind, reserving for garnish.

ASSEMBLY

Divide the apple mixture among six Martini glasses or small cups. Top with warm pastry cream. Bring to room temperature and refrigerate for at least 2 hours before serving. Top glasses with a simple decoration using the cinnamon stick and slices of lemon rind and serve.

*VEGAN ALTERNATIVE

500 ml (16 fl oz) soy milk

2½ tablespoons cornflour

Rind of ½ lemon

4 tablespoons sugar, plus 1 tablespoon for apples

½ vanilla bean, split and scraped lengthwise

10 saffron threads soaked in 1 tablespoon of hot water for 1 hour

———

Combine all the ingredients except the saffron and bring to a boil to thicken. When the cream coats the back of a spoon, gently mix in the saffron. Remove from the heat, cover with plastic film and cool to room temperature. Proceed as the original recipe.

MONTALI AVOCADO SURPRISE

A dessert notorious for keeping the Montali guests guessing until the end of the meal, this Brazilian avocado pudding is as delicious as it is perplexing.

Serves 8   (E)   *10 minutes & 25 minutes baking*

INGREDIENTS

5 bananas
6 tablespoons granulated sugar
Brown sugar to taste
Cinnamon to taste
2 tablespoons butter
2 ripe avocados
Juice of 2 lemons
1 kiwi fruit

———

Preheat the oven to Gas Mark 4/175°C/350°F. Peel four bananas and halve lengthwise. Place, cut side up, on a baking tray covered with buttered parchment paper. Sprinkle over 2 tablespoons of sugar, brown sugar and cinnamon and dot with the butter. Bake for 25 minutes or until golden brown and caramelised. Remove from the heat and cool.

Using a small knife, peel and core the avocados, reserving the stone. Purée in a blender with 4 tablespoons of sugar and the lemon juice. Taste for flavour and add more sugar or lemon if necessary, depending on the quality of the avocado. Place the core back in the mixture (to keep the avocado from discolouring), cover with plastic film and refrigerate until chilled.

Serve in martini glasses with slices of the remaining banana and kiwi fruit lining the rim and the caramelised bananas on the side.

The avocado must be fully ripe when preparing this dish. To speed the ripening process, wrap fruit in newspaper and store in a warm place until soft.

FRAGOLE allo ZABAIONE e PANNA

Fresh strawberries with zabaglione sauce and double cream. The best way to eat fresh strawberries during their season. The sweet zabaglione goes perfectly with the sharp fruit. A small layer of double cream will top everything off with class.

Serves 6 (E) *15 minutes & chilling time*

STRAWBERRIES

225 g (8 oz) fresh strawberries, destemmed

White wine, for rinsing fruit

Juice of ½ lemon

1 tablespoon cassis liqueur

1 tablespoon sugar

———

Up to 2 hours before serving, rinse the strawberries with the wine and quarter them. Toss with the lemon juice, cassis and sugar. Cover with plastic film and refrigerate.

Strawberries are rinsed with white wine to retain the beautiful colour of the fruit, as well as to enhance the flavour.

ZABAGLIONE

4 egg yolks

4 tablespoons sugar

2 tablespoons Grand Marnier or Marsala

2 tablespoons white wine

———

Whisk the egg yolks and sugar together in a medium saucepan until pale yellow. Mix in the liqueur and wine to combine. Cook in a double-boiler, stirring continuously, until thickened, about 5 minutes. Remove from the heat and cool over an ice bath (see page 21). Cover with plastic film so that the plastic is just touching the entire surface of the cream (this prevents the cream from creating a skin). Refrigerate.

TO SERVE

300 ml (10 fl oz) whipping cream

1 tablespoon icing sugar

———

Just before serving, whip the double cream with the icing sugar to soft peaks. Foam the zabaglione with a hand-held mixer until pale yellow. Serve in individual wine glasses with the zabaglione on the strawberries and a dollop of cream.

CHARLOTTE dell' ABATE

A fabulous dessert for which the literal translation is 'The Charlotte of the Abbot'. In the Italian tradition, the abbot was always served the best food as the head of the monastery. A kingly food.

Serves 12 (M) *60 minutes & 4 hours freezing & 1 hour thawing*

ZABAGLIONE

4 egg yolks
4 tablespoons sugar
4 tablespoons Marsala
4 tablespoons white wine

———

In a small saucepan away from the heat, whisk the egg yolks with the sugar until pale yellow. Whisk in the Marsala and wine and cook in a double boiler on a medium heat. Stir continuously for 5 minutes or until thickened. Immediately transfer to a bowl and cool over an ice bath (see page 21), stirring all the time. When the cream has cooled, cover with plastic film and refrigerate until needed.

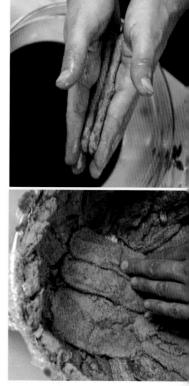

CHOCOLATE CHIP CREAM

350 ml (12 fl oz) double cream
3 tablespoons icing sugar with vanilla
150 g (5½ oz) bittersweet chocolate, chopped

———

Whip the cream with the icing sugar to soft peaks. Fold in the grated chocolate and refrigerate.

CAKE/ASSEMBLY

200 g (7 oz) sponge fingers
875 ml (29 fl oz) brewed espresso, room temperature
60 g (2 oz) amaretti biscuits, crushed coarsely

———

Line a medium-sized bowl with plastic film, allowing a substantial overhang around the sides. Soak two sponge fingers in the espresso. Place between your palms and gently squeeze out the liquid. If sections of the sponge are still crunchy, soak for a few more seconds. Line the bowl, two sponge fingers at a time, starting with the sides and covering the bottom last.

Pour half the zabaglione over the bottom and spread evenly with the back of a spoon. In a small bowl, drizzle espresso over half of the crushed amaretti biscuits to moisten, then sprinkle the crumbs over the zabaglione. Add half of the chocolate chip cream over the biscuits and spread evenly. Layer over more soaked sponge fingers to cover the cream. Repeat the layering process with the remaining ingredients. Fold in the overhanging sponge fingers around the rim, add one last level of soaked sponge fingers so the cream is completely enclosed, cover in plastic film and freeze for at least 4 hours.

Thaw for 1 hour before serving. Uncover the plastic, invert onto a large flat surface, remove the film and slice. Serve immediately.

CROCCANTE al PISTACCHIO

Layers of crunchy almond cookies filled with pistachio cream and wild berries. This decorative recipe has a succulent flavour and looks lovely. Great as the 'gran finale' of a posh meal.

Serves 6 **D** *45 minutes*

PASTRY CREAM

2 egg yolks

2 tablespoons granulated sugar

15 g (½ oz) flour

150 ml (5 fl oz) milk

40 g (1½ oz) pistachio nuts, peeled and ground

Whisk the egg yolks and sugar together in a small pot away from the heat until pale yellow, add the flour and mix well. In another pan, heat the milk. Just before it comes to a boil, add the milk to the yolk mixture, stirring continuously. Continue to whisk the cream for 5 minutes over a double boiler, or until thickened to the texture of creamy yoghurt. Remove from the heat and cool over an ice bath (see page 21). Set aside 2 tablespoons of ground pistachios for garnish and add the remainder to the cream. Cover with plastic film and refrigerate.

ALMOND COOKIES

15 g (½ oz) flour, plus extra for dusting

1½ egg whites

110 g (4 oz) icing sugar

1 oz butter (28 g) melted and cooled to room temperature

60 g (2 oz) slivered almonds

Preheat the oven to Gas Mark 4/180°C/350°F. Whisk all the cookie ingredients together, except the almonds, until smooth. Grease and flour a sheet of parchment paper or a silicon mat. Use a pastry brush to spread 1 tablespoon of batter into a thin 10 cm (4") circle. If the cookie batter is transparent on the sheet, add more. Fill the sheet with circles, top each with slivered almonds, sprinkle with extra icing sugar and bake in the oven for 4 minutes or until golden brown. Cool before removing delicately with a spatula. Continue until you have at least 18 nice cookies. Gently layer in an airtight container between paper towels or parchment paper.

MIXED BERRY SAUCE

90 g (3 oz) mixed berries

1 tablespoon brown sugar

1 teaspoon lemon juice

Mix all the ingredients together in a bowl and refrigerate until needed.

ASSEMBLY

18 fresh strawberries

White wine, for rinsing

6 blackberries

Mint leaves

Trim the stems from 12 strawberries and gently rinse with white wine. With stems still attached, halve six strawberries lengthwise. Stem and quarter the remainder into wedges. Wash the blackberries and set aside. Place a cookie on a plate and, with a pastry bag, pipe out 1 tablespoon of the pastry cream along one side of the cookie. Top with 1 teaspoon of mixed berry sauce. Arrange four strawberry wedges along the edge of the cookie. Place another cookie on a slant, with one edge against the pastry cream, so the appearance resembles an open sea shell. Repeat with more pastry cream, berry sauce and strawberry wedges and top with another cookie. Place two strawberry halves, one blackberry, and one mint sprig where the cookies meet (see picture). Sprinkle with icing sugar, reserved pistachios and one piece of Caramel Lace (see page 27).

BUDINO al COCCO con SALSA di PRUGNE

A Brazilian coconut pudding served with plum sauce. Requested again and again by guests… in a single sitting!

Serves 8 Ⓜ *25 minutes & 40 minutes for sauce*

COCONUT PUDDING*

120 ml (4 fl oz) coconut milk

8 tablespoons coconut flakes

125 g (4½ oz) sugar

500 ml (16 fl oz) milk

2 heaped tablespoons cornflour

¼ vanilla bean, split and scraped

100 ml (3½ fl oz) single cream

———

Submerge eight decorative ramekins or pudding cups, or one 13 cm (5") bundt pan, in a large bowl of water. Combine all pudding ingredients in a saucepan away from the heat and mix well until the cornflour dissolves completely. Place over a medium-low heat and bring the mixture to a boil, stirring constantly and cooking until the pudding sizzles and pulls away from the bottom of the pan. Invert the prepared pudding cups to drain away most of the water (but do not dry) and immediately pour the hot mixture in. The wetness of the cups will keep the pudding from adhering to the sides. Cool to room temperature, then refrigerate until ready to serve.

SAUCE

150 ml (5 fl oz) water

75 g (2¾ oz) sugar

Rind of ½ lemon, peeled in large strips

2 tablespoons lemon juice

———

Combine all sauce ingredients, except the plums and lemon juice, in a small pot and simmer for 40 minutes or until the liquid is reduced by half. Remove from the heat and cool completely. Remove the rind and add the lemon juice. Refrigerate.

TO SERVE

8 dried plums (not stoned)

———

Carefully invert the puddings, running a knife around the edges if necessary. Top each pudding with one plum and drizzle 2 tablespoons of sauce over the top. Serve immediately.

*VEGAN ALTERNATIVE

Switch the milk for soy milk and the single cream to soy cream. Follow the same procedure.

CROSTATINE di MANDORLE

Crostata is surely one of the most popular cakes in Italy. This fanciful variation is filled with sweet almonds instead of jam. Excellent for afternoon tea.

Serves 6   Ⓜ   *35 minutes & 30 minutes chilling*

DOUGH

400 g (14¼ oz) Italian '00' flour

150 g (3½ oz) sugar

2 teaspoons baking powder

200 g (7 oz) butter, at room temperature

1 whole egg

1 tablespoon Limoncello

Zest of 1 lemon

1 pinch salt

3 tablespoons water

———

On a flat surface, combine the flour, sugar and baking powder and make a well in the centre. Add the remaining ingredients into the well and work with your fingertips until a dough begins to form. Incorporate by cutting through the dough with a pastry cutter and rolling back together, three or four times, until the texture and colour is even, adding a little water if too dry. Wrap in plastic film and refrigerate for 30 minutes..

FILLING

300 g (11 oz) ground almonds

225 g (8 oz) sugar

2 whole eggs, lightly beaten

Zest of 1 lemon

65 ml (2¼ fl oz) water

———

Combine all the ingredients and mix well to cream. Set aside.

ASSEMBLY

Roll out two-thirds of the dough between two sheets of parchment paper into a 33 cm (13") wide disc. Remove the top sheet and carefully invert the dough over a 25 cm (11") non-stick pie tin. Gently press the dough into the edges and rim. Run a rolling pin over the rim to cut off excess dough and add the trimmings to the remaining third of the dough. Fill the pie with the almond mixture and spread smoothly with a spatula. Roll out the remaining dough between two sheets of parchment paper into a 30 cm (12") disc. Use a pastry cutter to cut into 1 cm (½") wide strips. Layer half the strips horizontally 1 cm (½") apart. Layer the remaining strips 1 cm (½") apart diagonally over the top. Gently press to seal where the strips meet the pie edge. Bake at Gas Mark 4/180°C/350°F for 20 minutes. Remove from the oven and cool completely. Slice and serve at room temperature with a sprinkling of icing sugar.

This same recipe can make 12 miniature pies, following the same method. To bake, lower the temperature to Gas Mark 3/170°C/325°F for 15 minutes.

BISCOTTO alla PANNA

A chocolate and whipped cream roulade that is this delicate and light can only be achieved with the highest quality cocoa powder. Very quick to make, it's a fabulous dessert.

Serves 10 (E) *20 minutes & 1 hour chilling*

CAKE

4 eggs, yolks and whites separated
5 tablespoons sugar
Pinch of salt
4 tablespoons unsweetened cocoa powder

———

Preheat the oven to Gas Mark 4/175°C/350°F. Butter a 35 x 35 cm (14 x 14") sheet of parchment paper and place on a baking tray.

Whisk the egg yolks and sugar together until they are pale yellow. Whisk the egg whites with the salt to stiff peaks. Fold into the yolks in three batches, fully incorporating each time. Sift in the cocoa powder and fold, being careful not to overwork the mixture. Pour the egg mixture over the parchment paper and, working quickly, spread it evenly with a spatula, covering the surface of the parchment. Bake in the oven for 7 minutes, or until it springs back to the touch. Avoid overcooking as the cake will become too hard and break. Remove and cool completely.

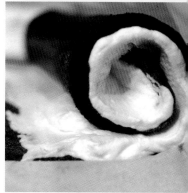

FILLING

350 ml (12 fl oz) double cream
2 tablespoons icing sugar
1 teaspoon vanilla extract

———

Whisk all the ingredients together to a soft peak.

ASSEMBLY

Lay the cake, still on the parchment sheet, on a flat work surface. With a spatula, spread the whipped cream evenly over the cake, leaving a 4 cm (1½") rim uncovered at the top. Using the parchment paper as a guide, roll the cake upwards from the bottom to the top until the seam of the cake is facing down. Carefully pull the cake off the paper and place on a long serving plate. Fill the ends with any remaining whipped cream and refrigerate for at least 1 hour before serving. Slice with a sharp knife so that the roulade holds its shape.

SOUFFLÉ di RICOTTA

A chocolate and ricotta cheese soufflé served with a Grand Marnier and basil cream. This is one of the most sophisticated desserts at the Country House Montali and always receives praise from guests.

Serves 8 Ⓓ *55 minutes & 1 hour freezing*

CHOCOLATE HEARTS

55 g (2 oz) 43% bittersweet chocolate, grated

35 ml (1¼ fl oz) single cream

Melt the chocolate and single cream together in a double boiler until combined. Cool to room temperature. Line a small plate with plastic film and scoop out teaspoon-sized portions. Freeze for at least 1 hour.

BASIL ZABAGLIONE

3 egg yolks
3 tablespoons sugar
6 tablespoons Grand Marnier

5 basil leaves
150 ml (5 fl oz) double cream

Whisk the egg yolks and sugar together in a small saucepan away from the heat until pale yellow. Add the Grand Marnier and cook in a double boiler, stirring, for 5 minutes or until thickened. Remove from the heat and cool over an ice bath (see page 21). Cover and refrigerate. Thirty minutes before serving, foam the zabaglione with a mixer. Finely chop the basil and whip the double cream to soft peaks. Fold both into the zabaglione and refrigerate.

SOUFFLÉ

Butter and sugar for ramekins
200 g (7 oz) ricotta
60 g (2 oz) honey
1½ quantity Lemon Strings (see page 29)
1 tablespoon lemon juice

1 egg yolk
40 g (1½ oz) sugar
2 full tablespoons cornflour
4 egg whites
Pinch of salt

Preheat the oven to Gas Mark 6/200°C/400°F. Butter eight ramekin cups or a silicon muffin pan and dust with granulated sugar. Bring a medium-sized pot of water to the boil. Beat the ricotta with a fork until very creamy. Mix in the honey, two-thirds of the Lemon Strings (finely chopped), lemon juice and egg yolk, mixing well after each addition while sifting in the sugar and cornflour as well. In a separate bowl, beat the egg whites and salt with a mixer to form stiff peaks. Fold gently into the ricotta mixture. Spoon 1 tablespoon of mixture into each baking cup. Remove the chocolate hearts from the freezer. Place a chocolate heart in the centre of each cup and top with another tablespoon of mixture. Place the cups in a baking pan with 5 cm (2") sides. Pour boiling water halfway up the sides of the cups and bake immediately for 17 minutes.

TO SERVE

Remove the soufflés from the oven and take out of the water. Gently invert one soufflé at a time onto a wide spatula, place on individual plates and serve immediately with the Basil Zabaglione, topping with the remainder of the Lemon Strings.

TORTA SACHER

The story of this famous dessert comes from Vienna in 1832 when the city was the capital of the Austro-Hungarian empire. For many years there has been a dispute over the real creator of the recipe. On the one hand was Franz Sacher, the young pastry chef of Prince Von Metternich Winnesburg, and on the other was Edward Demel, manager of the most famous pastry shop in the town, at that time owned by the Hotel Sacher.

Serves 16 Ⓜ *50 minutes & 15 minutes chilling*

CAKE

5 small eggs, at room temperature, separated
Pinch of salt
150 g (5½ oz) sugar
150 g (5 fl oz) sunflower oil
70 g (2½ oz) flour

4 tablespoons unsweetened cocoa
   powder
2 teaspoons baking powder
Pinch of vanilla
28 g (1 oz) ground almond flour
400 g (14 oz) apricot jam

Prepare an 28 cm (11") non-stick spring-form tin lined with parchment paper over the bottom. Preheat the oven to Gas Mark 4/175°C/350°F. Beat the egg yolks, salt and a third of the sugar together with a hand-held mixer until pale yellow. Pour in the oil in a steady stream, mixing constantly. In a separate bowl, sift the flour, cocoa, baking powder and vanilla together, then add in the almond flour. In another bowl, whip the egg whites with a hand-held mixer to stiff peaks, adding the remaining sugar halfway through. Add half to the yolk mixture. Sift the dry ingredients into the mix in four batches, gently incorporating after each addition. Mix in the remaining egg whites. Pour the batter into the tin and bake for 35 minutes. Cool completely.

ASSEMBLY

Carefully even the top layer of the cake with a serrated knife. Slice the cake horizontally into three equal layers. Remove the top two layers and spread a third of the apricot jam over the bottom layer. Top with a layer of cake and spread over a third more jam. Add the final layer of cake. Pass the remaining jam through a fine sieve, discard any solids and coat the top and sides of the cake with a thin layer of the smooth jam. Transfer the cake to a cake stand.

GLAZE

280 g (10 oz) 70% bittersweet chocolate
15 ml (½ fl oz) water

28 g (1 oz) sugar
90 ml (3 fl oz) double cream

Melt the chocolate in a double boiler. In a small saucepan, heat the water and sugar together until the sugar dissolves. Transfer to a bowl. Heat the cream to a boil and immediately pour into the syrup, whisking continously. Add the melted chocolate to the syrup and whisk quickly to incorporate well. The mixture will be bubbly. Rest for a few minutes until the glaze is completely smooth and bubble-free (test by coating the back of a spoon for a shiny and smooth texture). Pour the warm glaze evenly over the cake, covering the surface. With a spatula, spread the glaze over the top and sides and refrigerate for 15 minutes to set the glaze. Slice and serve.

Note: For a very traditional cake, reserve a small amount of the glaze in a piping bag with a very fine tip. After the cake has chilled briefly, write 'Sacher' on top of the cake with the reserved glaze.

VEGAN SACHER

This vegan version of the traditional dessert loses nothing in texture or flavour.

Serves 8 (M) *50 minutes & 15 minutes chilling*

CAKE

75 g (2½ oz) unsweetened cocoa powder

200 g (7½ oz) Italian '00' flour

200 g (7½ oz) sugar

½ teaspoon salt

1¼ teaspoons baking powder

1 teaspoon vanilla extract

80 ml (2½ fl oz) brewed espresso, cooled

100 ml (3½ fl oz) sunflower oil

2 tablespoons vinegar

210 ml (7 fl oz) soy milk

200 g (7 oz) apricot jam

———

Line an 20 cm (8") square baking tin with parchment paper with a 5 cm (2") overhang on all sides and grease lightly. Sift the dry ingredients together into a medium-sized bowl. In a larger bowl, stir the vanilla, coffee, oil and vinegar together. In three batches, sift the dry ingredients into the liquid, whisking well after each addition. Mix in the soy milk. Pour the batter into the baking tin, spread evenly and bake at Gas Mark 4/180°C/350°F for 35 minutes, or until a toothpick comes out clean from the middle. Cool completely in the pan.

The assembly is the same as for the traditional Sacher.

GANACHE

2 tablespoons unsweetened cocoa powder

3 tablespoons icing sugar

2 tablespoons warm espresso

2 tablespoons margarine, at room temperature

———

In a double boiler, combine the ganache ingredients and mix until shiny and even. Remove from the heat. While still warm, pour evenly over the cake and spread with a spatula or knife. Cool completely and chill for 15 minutes in the refrigerator before serving.

GELATI

Literally 'Colds'. Classic Italian ice creams. What better way to spend a hot summer afternoon with your friends than tasting a variety of these? Always a favourite with children. While these recipes call for the use of an ice-cream maker, they can be made efficiently without it. Follow the procedure as given, freeze the ice cream for 20 minutes in a large bowl, whisk vigorously for 1 minute until creamy, re-freeze and repeat twice.

Chocolate Ginger
Serves 8

125 ml (4¼ fl oz) milk	75 g (2½ oz) milk chocolate, grated
125 ml (4¼ fl oz) double cream	2 egg yolks
1 teaspoon ginger, peeled and grated	60 g (2 oz) sugar

Combine the milk, cream and ginger in a saucepan over a medium-high heat. Bring to a boil, turn off the heat and add the chocolate, stirring occasionally until melted. Meanwhile, in a second saucepan, whisk the egg yolks and sugar together until pale yellow. Pass the chocolate cream through a fine sieve directly into the egg mixture and whisk until well combined. Continue to whisk over a double boiler for three more minutes. Remove from the heat, cool over an ice bath and pass through a fine sieve once more. Run the cream through an ice cream or gelato machine for 30–40 minutes. Store in an air-tight container in the freezer for up to 1 week. (Note: For a basic Chocolate Gelato, leave out the ginger.)

Liquorice
Serves 8

½ teaspoon natural liquorice candies, chopped	300 ml (10 fl oz) milk
180 ml (6 fl oz) double cream	75 g (2½ oz) sugar

Combine all the ingredients in a double boiler over a low heat. Stir until the liquorice melts completely. Pour through a fine sieve to catch any remaining solid particles. Cool over an ice bath, pass through a fine sieve another time and whisk to foam lightly. Run through an ice cream or gelato machine. Store in an air-tight container in the freezer for up to 1 week.

Strawberry
Serves 8

1 pint fresh strawberries, stems removed	100 g (3½ oz) sugar
White wine for rinsing	150 ml (5 fl oz) double cream
Juice of 1 lemon	100 ml (3½ fl oz) milk

Rinse the strawberries gently in white wine and purée in a blender. Pour through a sieve and discard any solids. Pour into a medium-sized bowl and add the lemon juice and sugar. Mix until well incorporated. Add the double cream and milk into the strawberry mixture and whisk until the mixture is creamy. Run through a gelato or ice cream machine for 30–40 minutes. Store in an airtight container in the freezer for up to 1 week.

Amaretto and Apricot
Serves 8

5 dried apricots, chopped
Grand Marnier, for rinsing
125 ml (4¼ fl oz) double cream
180 ml (6 fl oz) milk

55 g (2 oz) sugar
125 g (4¼ oz) fresh apricot purée
2 teaspoons lemon juice
8 amaretti biscuits, crushed

———

Combine the dried apricots and enough Grand Marnier to cover them in a small saucepan. Heat for 2 minutes, drain and set aside the apricots. Beat the cream and milk with the sugar, apricot purée and lemon juice. Run through a gelato or ice cream machine for 30–40 minutes. When the gelato is nearly done, fold in the liqueur-infused apricots and the crushed amaretti biscuits. Finish running the ice cream machine and freeze. Store in an airtight container in the freezer for up to 1 week.

The apricots can be replaced by the same quantity of peaches.

Lemon
Serves 8

200 ml (6½ fl oz) milk
200 ml (6½ fl oz) double cream
Juice of 3 lemons

130 g (4½ oz) sugar
4 tablespoons Limoncello

———

Whisk all ingredients together until airy. Run through an ice cream or gelato machine. Store in an airtight container in the freezer for up to 1 week.

Avocado
Serves 8

2 ripe avocados, peeled and stones removed
Juice of 1 lemon
5 tablespoons sugar

125 ml (4¼ fl oz) double cream
125 ml (4¼ oz) milk
90 ml (3 oz) sweetened condensed milk

———

Purée the avocados in a blender with the lemon and sugar. Add the remaining ingredients and blend for an additional minute. Run through an ice cream or gelato machine for 30–40 minutes. Store in an airtight container in the freezer for up to 1 week.

Coconut
Serves 8

200 ml (7 fl oz) coconut milk
150 ml (5 fl oz) double cream
150 ml (5 fl oz) milk

4 tablespoons sugar
1 whole vanilla bean, split and scraped

———

Beat all the ingredients together. Pour through a sieve and run through an ice cream or gelato machine for 30–40 minutes. Store in an airtight container in the freezer for up to 1 week.

Mango
Serves 8

2 mangoes, peeled and stones removed
125 ml (4¼ fl oz) double cream

125 ml (4¼ fl oz) milk
150 ml (5 fl oz) sweetened condensed milk

———

Purée the mangoes in a blender and pour through a sieve to catch the solids. Whip the juice with the remaining ingredients. Run through an ice cream or gelato machine for 30–40 minutes. Store in an airtight container in the freezer for up to 1 week.

Mint and Basil
Serves 8

12 mint leaves, washed and dried
10 basil leaves, washed and dried
360 ml (12 fl oz) milk

360 ml (12 fl oz) double cream
5 egg yolks
90 g (3 oz) sugar

———

Freeze the mint and basil leaves for 10 minutes. Chop and freeze again until needed. Bring the milk and cream to a boil, then remove from the heat. Meanwhile, in a medium-sized saucepan whisk the egg yolks with the sugar until pale yellow. Pour the milk into the eggs while whisking constantly. Cook the mixture in a double boiler until thickened to the point of coating a wooden spoon, approximately 5 minutes. Cool completely over an ice bath and sieve. Mix in the frozen herbs. Run through an ice cream or gelato machine for 30–40 minutes. Store in an airtight container in the freezer for up to 1 week.

Rum Raisin
Serves 8

2 egg yolks
110 g (4 oz) sugar
250 ml (8 fl oz) milk

150 ml (5 fl oz) double cream
5 tablespoons raisins
Rum

———

Beat the egg yolks and sugar together in a medium-sized bowl until pale yellow. Combine the milk and cream in a saucepan over a medium-high heat. Bring to a boil, turn off the heat and pass the milk and cream through a sieve into the egg mixture. Continue to whisk over a double boiler for 3 minutes. Remove from the heat, cool over an ice bath and run through a gelato or ice cream machine for 30–40 minutes. Meanwhile, rinse the raisins and rehydrate by simmering in enough rum to cover them. Drain and cool completely. When the ice cream is almost done, add the raisins with 1 tablespoon of fresh rum. Store in an airtight container in the freezer for up to 1 week.

Hazelnut – Vegan
Serves 4

300 ml (10 fl oz) soy milk
60 ml (2 fl oz) soy cream
70 g (2½ oz) chopped hazelnuts

3 teaspoons hazelnut butter
2 tablespoons brown sugar

———

Mix all the ingredients together in a double boiler until the sugar has completely dissolved. Cool over an ice bath, then pour through a sieve. Whip lightly for 30 seconds, then run through a gelato or ice cream machine for 30–40 minutes. Transfer to an airtight container and keep in the freezer for up to 1 week.

Chocolate – Vegan
Serves 4

210 ml (7 fl oz) soy milk
100 ml (3½ fl oz) soy cream

55 g (2 oz) fine quality bittersweet chocolate
3 tablespoons sugar

———

Mix all the ingredients together in a double boiler until the sugar has completely dissolved. Cool over an ice bath. Pour through a sieve. Whip lightly for 30 seconds, then run through a gelato or ice cream machine for 30–40 minutes. Transfer to an airtight container and keep in the freezer for up to 1 week.

Carrot, Orange and Limoncello Sorbet
Serves 8

2 carrots, peeled and grated
250 ml (8 fl oz) orange juice
270 ml (9 fl oz) water
3 tablespoons lemon juice

Zest of 1 organic lemon
3 tablespoons Limoncello
85 g (3 oz) sugar

———

Purée all the ingredients together in a blender. Run through a gelato or ice cream machine for 30–40 minutes. Transfer to an airtight container and keep in the freezer for up to 1 week.

This sorbet is wonderful to clean and refresh the palate between courses.

interact socially or get to know each other during the event, but later that night, as they sat together at an Indian restaurant, they laughed as old friends and shared hilarious knee-slapping stories of their own Montali experiences. Spending so many months with Malu and Alberto in the lifestyle of the Country House had formed a unique bond among them, despite their diverse backgrounds. While the prospect of going to London had been exciting, they all knew they were not there on holiday. After years apart, they still felt a strong commitment to Malu and Alberto, two people they had come to know and love as family. It was their devotion to them and Montali for which they put forth so much of their time and energy. It was stressful, frustrating and exhausting to the point of hilarity. But to them, it was just like old times.

ANECDOTE ON RUNNING AN HOTEL

Henry Togna once said: "An hotelier must be a diplomat, a democrat, an autocrat, an acrobat, and a doormat. He must have the facility to entertain Prime Ministers, princes of industry, pickpockets, gamblers, bookmakers, pirates, philanthropists, popsies and prudes." He meant, of course, that it is a necessity in this kind of profession always to be ready with an appropriate answer under any circumstance.

As I started running restaurants and entertaining people at a very young age, I have been trying to learn this all my life, even if not always successfully. Still I would hope I have developed a quick thinking reaction while conversing with others, because that is often what you are involved with in hotel life. There are always many people around and many conversations going on.

Nevertheless the day in which two Californian ladies checked into my hotel, I ended up, for the first time of my working life absolutely speechless. As one of the two women was quite a bit older than the other, I politely asked if they were sisters. A good hotelier would never make the mistake of asking if they were mother and daughter, as if they were actually sisters he would be in trouble. As a trying-to-be charming Italian, I asked them so, but, to my major surprise, I received an honest and unexpected answer from the oldest lady: "Oh,

no. We are lesbians!!" And myself: "Wow, congratulations… no oops." What can you answer to someone, absolutely unknown to you, who tells you about her private life on first meeting? But now I have learned my lesson. When I see two ladies with an age difference, I don't ask anymore "Are you sisters?" I just directly ask: "Are you lesbians?" and I have seen it work! Well, hotel life. "How many stories behind those walls!" Ours is a small country resort thankfully, with a very good clientele.

People don't 'pass by' our place as it is 8 km in the middle of nowhere. All our guests have really made an effort to book, fly, drive and come all the way up to Montali. All this creates a very friendly and elegant crowd quite happy to have a nice relaxing time, conversing with other people and enjoying the best food. People are generally not here for a single night in a marathon of 'touring Europe in 15 days'. The attraction of the food, moreover, tends to bring people from many different countries and with many different views, as well as those with a specific diet. We work for example with many Jewish people, both from Israel and the USA. I find it interesting, the Kosher approach to vegetarianism.

We cater to specific tailor-made diets for many other 'groups': vegan, people with gluten problems, dairy allergies, egg-free diets, and many

new modern allergies and food intolerances as well.

We had a case of a client intolerant to 90 percent of the possible products in the world, being allergic to a very common element present in nearly everything. We could only use six ingredients in total to make all her food. Of course my wife, every day for a week, wanted to create the usual four full gourmet courses especially for her! But to keep varying four courses for seven nights, with only six ingredients both for sweet and for savoury dishes was definitely not easy!

That was a real culinary challenge that later became a big lesson for us. I remember the emotions when, at the end of her stay, the nice lady came to thank my wife and the kitchen staff for the effort of making such varied food, in such quantities and with that level of difficulty.

All this just for her! Sadly she added how she had not been able to go to any restaurants for a good 13 years because of her illness. The chefs felt immediately proud of their job and no one felt tired that night in spite of the amount of hard work that been done.

I still remember my wife telling me months later how interesting she had found that specific culinary experience. To have been forced, for a full week, to cook only with such a limited number of products had got her involved in a kind of molecularly different food dimension. Any taste she wanted to create had to be produced with only those few ingredients. This was highly unusual considering that we usually use at least 26 different kinds of cheese in our kitchen. Yes, only cheese! You can imagine that the number of entire ingredients in a professional kitchen can go up to hundreds. She found she really had to enter the molecular inner world of those six materials to try to develop as many new tastes as possible if she wanted to succeed in the challenge. Of course you have to develop to always keep changing the taste of the same product.

But she discovered some new, interesting means of doing it.

She generally started by using one single ingredient of the six. Then she would try to modify it by heating the ingredient, by shaking it, by roasting it, by stirring it, by shaking and heating it, then by mixing it with another product and then again heating or shaking or...

It was no more the usual recipe, such as 1 kg tomato and 2 kg potato, which you just cook and mix together.

Here it was more like: "three warm molecules of corn oil heated at 45°, mixed with other two molecules that have been instead grilled at 170° and then mixed with half the sugar already steamed at 120°."

Wow, pure alchemy! As a professional chef you would never tend to cook like this, as you can achieve the same taste much more quickly using more ingredients. But not having the ingredients, that was the only way. For a good chef like Malu, it was a real 'taste sublimation test'. It was a real journey through palate, brain and stomach to check how the brain could fool the palate with the help of the stomach! This was a real last goal in culinary life. If that gentle lady has been thankful to my wife

for such food, my wife has surely been even more grateful for giving her the chance to undergo such a journey in the culinary sciences.

Some satisfaction, some hard times – that's how life goes. I am just happy that we never had to face any 'terrible' customers in our little resort. Try just to imagine, for example, how difficult times can be working in top quality hotels. So often the aim of big spending guests is to give the hardest time to the people working there, as a kind of personal gratification and justification for spending so much. The manager of the Mandarin Hotel once wrote that the most demanding customer of his working life had been a pop star who didn't like ....the wallpaper of the room.

The problem came when she wanted it to be changed before the end of the day. You can imagine.

Our guests are so varied; none, luckily, so demanding. A lot of musicians, artist, intellectuals, gourmets.

Many nationalities as well. In the kitchen last year we have been speaking English, Polish, American, Korean, Slovakian, Spanish, Portuguese, Swedish and eventually Italian too. My son was driven mad.

Some customers have definitely left nice memories with us. Some have left us with a good laugh. I remember a couple from the UK coming to dinner with a big bottle of Moet et Chandon for us and the staff, as they had just heard that Montali had been choosen for a BBC holiday programme.

A Californian lady once made my day when I went to announce that food was ready. She called me to a corner to tell me privately that she was ....a vegetarian, but she would have been happy to eat even a simple salad as she didn't want to create any inconvenience to my staff. She had booked three nights in our resort and didn't notice the place was fully vegetarian. That was not a bad accident considering

how the lady ended up loving the food. She made my day full of fun and the chefs made her three days worthwhile with their food.

Of course, we sometimes get the opposite cases, people booking without noticing the place was exclusively vegetarian. I recall an elderly couple from Belgium, speaking very little English (and of course no Italian). The husband started to shout at his wife in front of me when I told them that the food was only vegetarian. She had chosen the hotel from a tour operator's catalogue, but she had thought it was only an option to the regular food and so the gentleman got really mad with her (and almost with me as well) for having booked here. The funny part was when he started to enjoy the food so much that he literally licked every plate. I was almost saying, "hey, weren't you the person who didn't want to eat here at all?" When you work with people, you don't always get only the good ones.

But you must always try to please everyone. That is your only goal.

That is why you are there. The important thing at the end, is that, when someone leaves your door, he will take something with him: hopefully some good energy, perhaps some nice food, definitely a pleasant relaxing memory. I always teach my waitresses that the most important thing to leave a client with is a beautiful warm smile. Arm yourself with a good sense of humour and you will manage to succeed, smiling through your life.

There is no better sentence to conclude the book than what Daniel said once in the kitchen: "my favourite vegetable is bacon!!" That's the philosophy of how to work in a vegetarian hotel.

And again, as Mr. Togna said: "The hotelier must be outside, inside, offside, glorified, sanctified, crucified, stupefied, cross-eyed – and if he is not the strong, silent type, there is always suicide."

A.M.

THE VEGETERRAEAN